the *Bible*

or the *Axe*

# the Bible or the Axe

### one man's dramatic escape from persecution in the Sudan

# William O. Levi

**MOODY PUBLISHERS**
CHICAGO

Library of Congress Cataloging-in-Publication Data

Levi, William O.
    The Bible or the axe : one man's dramatic escape from persecution in the Sudan / by William O. Levi.
        p. cm.
    Originally published: Enumclaw, WA : WinePress Pub., 2004.
    ISBN-13: 978-0-8024-1138-9
        1. Levi, William O.  2. Christian biography—Sudan.
3. Christian biography—United States.  I. Title.

BR1725.L435A3 2005
276.24'0825'092—dc22

                                                      2005009860

ISBN: 0-8024-1138-X
ISBN-13: 978-0-8024-1138-9


1 3 5 7 9 10 8 6 4 2

*Printed in the United States of America*

*This book is dedicated to*

*my beloved wife, Hannah,*
*and our three olive shoots,*
*Abijah, Nechemyah, and Hadassah;*
*and to the memory of my beloved parents,*
*Ajjugo and Anna Levi;*
*and my childhood spiritual mentors,*
*maternal grandparents*
*Reverend Andrew and Lydia Vuni Wale*
—William Levi

*To the many around the world*
*who suffer for their beliefs*
—A. F. Chai

# Contents

# *Acknowledgments*

THANKS TO A. F. Chai, who donated greater than a thousand hours of "spare" time over a period of two-and-a-half years to bring my story to life. Without a ghostwriter to dig up facts, review endless piles of notes, and conduct interviews, this book could not have been completed. Thanks to Grace Fallon for transcribing five audiotapes of my testimony. Thanks to Monica Rizzo for entering my testimony into a computerized format.

I would like to thank my many friends and spiritual mentors who have encouraged me to move forward with this book, including Paul Liben, Michael Fallon, Scott Davis, Bruce Boucard, Pastor David Liebherr, Vic Eliason, Gary Selman, Bill Rizzo, and Rabbi Jonathan Cahn.

A special thanks to my brothers Michael, Joseph,

and Benjamin and their families for assisting me with family history and photography. Thanks to my lovely sisters Angela, Jemima, Rebecca, Rose, and Merriam as well as their families for gracing the family photo. I love you all.

Thanks to my good friend Michael Longwa and my cousin John Moi for all of your faithfulness and encouragement. Thanks to all of the staff members of Operation Nehemiah and their families. This book is your story too.

I am eternally grateful to the many individuals who have supported me over the years, many of whom are mentioned in this book. And, of course, I cannot forget to mention the love, support, and prayers of my wife, Hannah, and her parents, Robert and Ruth Kirkman.

May the Lord continue to bless the anonymous brother who originally sponsored the publication of this book. Without his generosity and kindness, it would not have been possible to print this book. He has been used of God in this ministry.

# Preface

*AND THEY SAID unto me, The remnant that are left of the captivity there in the province are in great affliction and reproach: the wall of Jerusalem also is broken down, and the gates thereof are burned with fire.* —Nehemiah 1:3

It was hot and so very dry. The little girl kept on walking, then crawling, knowing only that she must escape the horror that lay behind. Foot by agonizing foot she traveled, ever aware of the scorching heat of dry air entering her tiny lungs with each breath. No tears flowed from her large, dark eyes—there was not enough moisture for such a luxury. The tears flowed inside of her mind and caught at her throat like the talons of a great bird.

"Mama," she whispered, but that was all. There

was no strength left to speak to the rocks and dirt and twisted brush. There were no words left to cry out to the God her family had once depended on. She wondered vaguely if God had died too, along with her mama and papa and older brothers and sisters.

If only the pictures in her memory would stop playing over and over again.

The day had begun like any other, with Mama singing softly and preparing the family's meager breakfast over a small fire. Papa had gone out hunting with Big Brother, and Big Sister was playing with the baby. Life was not easy, but Mama and Papa believed that God would provide food for His children, and they were thankful for what they had.

Mama had looked at her that morning and smiled. "Are you awake, little sleepy girl?"

She had scooted over to the fire to give her mama a hug. Mama gave her a bite of breakfast, a special taste just for her. Mama would probably eat one less bite of breakfast to make up for it. She remembered that taste of porridge, and her stomach burned with hunger. She never got a chance to eat the rest of her breakfast.

Mama stopped singing, and the wooden spoon dropped into the pot. She could picture that spoon falling into the porridge. It was like slow motion. Then she heard the shouts. Papa and the other men were running back to the village, yelling for their families to run. Run and hide—but where?

Mama grabbed the baby and ran outside in time to see Papa's face just before he was cleft in two by the swords of the jihad soldiers. He fell slowly, like the wooden spoon, as his own blood wet the dry earth. She heard her mama scream, "Yeshua, save us!"

As her mother sank to her knees, the baby clutched to her breast, she was surrounded by a swarm of soldiers.

The little girl ran. She ran without stopping. She ran without feeling the thorny sharpness of the dry underbrush. She ran until her body could no longer go on, and then she collapsed into a stand of tall savannah grass. Through the musky scent of the sun-scorched grass, she smelled something else. Her village was burning.

She hid in the grass until the noise of the jihad soldiers stopped. Then it was quiet.

For a moment, she wondered if she were the only person from her village left alive. Then she remembered Papa's voice yelling, "Run!"

She got back up and started running. She ran southeast, toward the mountains. Across the mountains somewhere was Kenya. If she kept running, she would get there.

The little girl was tiny, and it was difficult to tell how old she was. Perhaps she was six or seven, perhaps eight or nine. She kept on walking, then crawling. The bite of porridge she had eaten had long since been used up in her struggle to survive. How could she go on?

She could hardly feel anything. She dreamed that she was walking through Kenya. *Are Mama and Papa in Kenya?* She was supposed to run there. Perhaps she was already there. Perhaps she could rest now.

As she sank to the ground, she did not escape the watchful eyes of the circling birds. They sharpened their talons with hungry beaks and began slowly drifting toward the ground.

\* \* \*

It was June of 1993. I stared at the photo in the newsmagazine, aware that my breath was coming in short, stabbing gasps. I saw a beautiful little child—alone and exhausted—haunted by vultures. Her journey was over.

I allowed the magazine to slip from my fingers as I trembled with sorrow for Africa's lost daughter.

"God," I said aloud, "how can this happen?"

I stood and paced the floor, willing myself not to cry as floods of memories washed over my consciousness. As I passed a mirror that hung on the wall, I stopped and stared. The face staring back at me was a face I no longer knew. It was an African face, like that of the little girl in the magazine. It was a face that knew the terror of South Sudan; and yet it was a well-fed face, clean-shaven and framed by a neat haircut. The young man I saw was dressed in clothing suited to a successful American engineering school graduate.

*Why did God allow me to escape the horror?* I could not erase the image of the little girl from my mind. Rage boiled inside of me like poison as I thought of the evil men who would reduce a child to carrion.

*What can I do?*

Slowly, the questions that burned in my mind started making sense. Maybe God had spared my life for a reason. Perhaps God meant for me to do something to help the children of Sudan. But what did He want me to do? I already had big plans for my life.

War and persecution had marred my own life. I had endured much before I ultimately made my escape to the Land of the Free. I had struggled to earn my way through college and had recently been rewarded with an engineering degree. The future was bright. It was finally my turn to experience a life of happiness and success.

*After all I have been through, don't I deserve it?* I reasoned. I had tasted the American Dream, and I wanted to eat it up. I often pictured myself driving home from church with wife and children in tow, laughing and enjoying the richness of God's blessings here in the United States. Of course, I would still be a devout Christian, doing good, raising a fine family, and serving in the church. Yes, God would be proud. Wouldn't He?

*I was hungry, and you gave Me no meat.*

The little girl's emaciated frame returned to my mind.

*I was thirsty, and you gave Me no drink.*

Her eyes were glazed and sunken as she crawled across the parched wilderness.

*I was a stranger, and you did not take Me in.*

I never knew her, but she was most likely from a Christian family, and that made her a member of my own household. How could I live a life of comfort and safety in America without caring deeply for my wounded brothers and little sisters? How could I allow myself to be moved by this young girl's suffering and then return to my own pleasant life?

I knew God was speaking to my heart, but I resisted. I wanted to put the past behind me—and put my head in the sand. I wished I could forget about the evil persecution and the desperate neediness of millions of people. But I could not.

"Lord," I prayed as earnestly as I knew how, "please show me what You want me to do. Whatever it is, I will do it."

A sense of peace came over me, and I knew that my heart and my will were heading in the right direction. I didn't realize how many struggles lay ahead, but I knew God would be with me. I picked up the newsmagazine from where it had landed on the floor and determined that I would read it—no matter how painful it might be.

Accompanying the photo essay was a story about the Sudanese orphans that American journalists had termed "the Lost Boys," after the parentless boys in the children's classic *Peter Pan*. But this story was not from a Disney film. Young children whose families had been slaughtered by jihad warriors wandered alone through Sudan's vast wilderness, facing unspeakable danger and hardship. Children who had seen fathers and mothers brutally murdered, sisters raped, and brothers burned alive ran until they could run no more. Some were eaten by jackals. Some died alone of starvation, leaving only bones picked clean by the buzzards. Miraculously, some made it out to tell their stories to the stunned journalists.

As I read their story, an uncomfortable sensation came over me. It was a feeling I had felt before, when I received news of my own father's murder at the hands of these same Islamic extremists. Was it vengeance? Was it hatred? The taste of it was bitterness in my mouth. I had escaped from Sudan just before the persecution of Christians rose to a fever pitch. I had seen it coming, and so had my father. My father, a messianic Jew, was a man I had admired and loved with all my heart. When I fled the country, I suspected I might never see him again. My suspicions were correct.

It had been November of 1987. One month earlier, I had experienced a disturbing dream. I was living in Lyon, France, at the time and attended a church run by an American missionary. I don't recall the details of the dream, but I remember a very vivid sense of urgency to pray for my family. I was so disquieted by the dream that I stood before the church to ask that they pray immediately, because my family was in grave danger. The church was faithful to intercede on their behalf.

Four weeks passed. I will never forget the letter I received that November day. It was from my cousin Samuel, who had been living in Kenya for some time. Corom, my family's village, had been burned to the ground by the jihad extremists on October 21. The people were exterminated and their homes destroyed.

Miraculously, my mother, brothers, and sisters

all escaped. They were camped out near the Ugandan border. My cousin chose his next words carefully, because he knew the heartbreak they would bring. My dear *abba*—my father, Ajjugo Levi—had been killed.

The thin paper, *par avion,* fluttered to the floor of my apartment. It drifted down slowly, like a leaf in the desert. My heart could feel its brittle substance. Now, six years later, the feeling had returned.

*"Vengeance is mine; I will repay, saith the Lord."*

That verse came to mind pretty readily. *Okay, God, go for it,* I thought. *Give those terrorists what they deserve.*

But then another verse came: *"Love your enemies. . . ."*

*God, You know I'm just not ready for that one. How can I love the people who killed my father and forced my mother into exile again? How can I love the people who were responsible for atrocities against peaceful families and helpless children? It isn't humanly possible.*

*"With God all things are possible. . . ."*

I got the message. But what did it look like for me, a Christian, to love my enemies? I needed a handle on what that sort of love really meant.

I knew that while we were yet sinners, and therefore enemies of God, Christ died for us. That is the ultimate example of unconditional agape love. The Islamic extremists had harmed my people and me. They were my enemies. And yet God commanded me to love them. I knew this could not be an emotional love, a love born of friendship and community. It would have to be a supernatural love, an agape love. It would have to be a decision that I make each and every day. I could *decide* to love them by praying for them regularly. I could *decide* to love them by refusing to seek vengeance. I could *decide* to love them by sharing the gospel message with them. I know that God's love is real love, whether or not I "feel" it.

Again, I felt a sense of peace; I knew that God was working in my heart to bring me to the place He wanted me to be. The remnant of my people was in great affliction and reproach. The gates of Corom and countless other villages in southern Sudan had been burned with fire. As in the days of Nehemiah, the walls of our protection were broken down.

*God,* I prayed, *please give me Your heart of forgiveness. Make me an instrument of Your peace and healing.*

This is my story.

# Chapter 1

# Exile

THE YEAR 1964 was a turbulent one. The eyes of the world were on Leonid Brezhnev as he assumed leadership of the Soviet Union, and on Lyndon Johnson as he escalated U.S. support to South Vietnam. While the newsmakers focused on the cold war, the Beatles "invaded" the States on *The Ed Sullivan Show*. The Western world, busy with other concerns, was barely aware of the unrest sweeping the African continent.

Colonial rule was ending for many African nations, and several African states gained their independence from European control. Rival factions seeking to gain power created tensions in many regions, sparking military confrontations and ethnic conflict. Corruption and violence were commonplace as each group promoted its own self-interest.

Sudan, the largest country in Africa, had been "liberated" from Great Britain ten years prior, and was still in political turmoil. The northern region of Sudan was predominantly Arab and Muslim, while the southern region was mainly African and Christian. Under British rule, religious and ethnic differences had been controlled by carefully isolating the northern and southern regions from one another.

The English government, growing ever more sensitive to Arab criticism of their management of the "southern problem," made a disastrous decision as they withdrew their colonial administration. Even though they knew that northern and southern regions were fundamentally incompatible, they determined that the whole of Sudan should be governed as one country. And so, Great Britain handed over the reins of leadership to the northern Arabs.

Predictably, the new regime replaced several hundred British colonial officials with northern Muslims. Violence erupted as the southerners rebelled, and the two regions of the new independent republic were plunged into conflict. Outnumbered, the southern freedom fighters were no match for the guerilla-style warfare of the northern Arabs.

The Muslim leader General Ibrahim Abboud, hoping to cut off the spread of Christianity, expelled all of the Western missionaries. It was the prelude to increased persecution of anyone who refused to convert to Islam.

This was the violent world into which I was born.

## Refugee Days

My mother delivered me beneath the spreading branches of a tree, with only the help of a midwife. I was the seventh among twelve siblings—five boys and seven girls. One of my sisters and two of my brothers died in infancy.

Our home was in the small village of Moli on the eastern bank of the Nile River in the equatorial district. My parents, Ajjugo and Anna Levi, were messianic Hebrews of the tribe of Levi, the son of Jacob to whom the hereditary priesthood had been entrusted.

In 1965, a year after my birth, the situation in Sudan became increasingly unstable. The war escalated and spread from the larger population centers out into the countryside. No one was safe. Our future was uncertain. Churches were burned, schools closed, and crops destroyed. The parents in our community feared for the safety of their families, and many people determined to escape from southern Sudan across the border into Uganda. Late that year, my parents decided that the time had come to leave their beloved homeland. With heavy hearts, they set about the difficult task of moving to Uganda.

The trip was perilous. The country of Sudan is nearly one million square miles, about the size of western Europe. Unlike Europe, however, there was no infrastructure in place across the vast interior— no roads to travel and no means of transportation. Families, often with several small children, were forced to hike the African wilderness on foot for hundreds of miles, struggling to cross rapid rivers and to avoid predators—both animal and human. Older children helped to carry younger ones over the treacherous terrain. My parents trusted that God would be with us, just as He had been with the Israelites as they wandered through the wilderness so long ago.

I do not remember the trip to Uganda, but I do know that God was faithful to my family. We were able to settle temporarily in Atyak, in northern Uganda. Although safe from the war in Sudan, things were nonetheless difficult. We did not speak the Ugandan language, and the culture and environment were foreign to us.

The United Nations descended on the country to set up refugee camps for the Sudanese people. My parents, however, were suspicious and did not wish to be detained in any sort of camp. Sudan's civil war had stirred up the specter of slavery, and my father did not want us to become victims. My family had firsthand knowledge of slave-raiding Arabs who kidnapped African children and sold them into bondage. Arab slavers had murdered my great-grandfather; and his wife, my great-grandmother, was taken as a slave. She was pregnant at the time with my grandfather, Karan Levi, and she was determined that her child would be free. Emboldened by her faith, she made a daring escape just in time to deliver a healthy baby boy.

The British had outlawed the practice of slave raiding, but the Islamists imposed no such restrictions. The large groups of Africans who huddled helplessly in refugee camps provided irresistible targets for kidnapping, mass murder, and other abuses. My parents refused to live in such a vulnerable situation, so they decided to settle in the small village of Abalo Kodi, in Atyak, Uganda. My father had an uncle who had moved to Abalo Kodi many years prior, and it was good to know someone in the new land.

My first memories as a child are those of growing up as a refugee in Uganda, but I didn't think of myself as a "refugee" because my parents provided us with the stability of their love and worked hard to build a home for us without the help of the UN camps. I knew that I had been born in the Sudan, and that our family would return there someday. But I didn't know how distant that day would be. For nearly ten years, our family would have to make the best of a bad situation.

## Pillars of Strength

My parents were farmers, hardworking and industrious. But the land in the Abalo Kodi region was not fertile, and the population was too dense. The overcrowding brought about by the refugee crisis made the area untenable for long-term living. There was simply no way to grow the food necessary to support a family.

My parents were soon forced to move on, trusting God to provide a place for us. With fervent prayer and careful inquiry, my father learned of a region near Mount Ambuluwa, where the soil was virgin and unspoiled, an ideal area for growing crops. So, we set off into the untamed Ugandan wilderness, away from the safety of Abalo Kodi, with nothing but willpower and strong faith to sustain us.

My father's name, Ajjugo, meant "pillar" in our native tongue, and it was prophetic of his character. He was strong, tall, and upright. Although he had no formal education, he was a master farmer and builder. He was also a strong spiritual leader, and his opinion was well regarded in the community.

My mother, Anna, was his partner in everything, and she completed him in every way. She had an inner beauty that radiated through her life and in her actions. Mama was gracious, hospitable, and tough —she and my father made a great team. Mother was not afraid of settling in the Ugandan wilderness.

God blessed me with two wonderful parents, and I loved them very much. I still cherish my first memories of my parents working together to open the wilderness, building a home and a productive farm with nothing but sweat and prayers. And it was a beautiful home. It was as if God had re-created the garden of Eden right there in Uganda. Every type of animal and plant flourished in the unspoiled jungle.

We built our home atop a hill beside a huge tamarind tree. This leafy giant grew to over fifty feet tall, and its pretty yellow flowers gave way in season to a wild edible fruit. I remember that its broad boughs provided a dense shade, suitable for family gatherings away from the hot equatorial sun. Tamarind fruit, called *iti* in the Madi tongue, changes from green to brown when it is ripe; and the juicy flesh is both sugary and sour. I loved to peel away the fibrous brown pod and suck out the juice, spitting out the seeds as I ate. Mama knew it was an excellent source of vitamins, and she used it to flavor porridge and also for medicinal purposes.

When work was done, I learned to climb in the sturdy limbs of our tamarind tree. My brothers and sisters could play hide-and-seek among the green branches. Sometimes we would even climb to the top to get a better view if we heard an airplane fly overhead. Living next to that tree was like living next to a park—complete with a playground and a free picnic basket. It kept us younger children busy while Mother and Father set about the serious business of home construction.

Building a home with no nails, materials, or power tools is a skill passed down from father to son. I remember watching my father select the proper trees to build our new home. The dense tropical forest was rich with trees, reeds, bamboo, and herbs to be used in the building process.

"How about this tree, Father?" I asked, pointing out a sturdy-looking trunk. Father smiled and reached out to strip away a portion of the bark. Every part of life was an opportunity to teach, and Father was preparing a lesson for me.

"Fine-looking bark, isn't it?" he said as he peeled away the loose outer layer. "People tend to judge by appearances, but God looks upon our hearts."

As the bark was loosened and fell away, I could see the telltale burrow marks of insect infestation. The tree was rotten inside!

"When you build your house, Son, be sure to use the type of wood that will stand the test of time. If you don't, it will collapse and you will be right back where you started."

I watched with fascination as Father selected and cut the finest wood and reeds from the richness of the forest. When the materials were assembled, the process of construction could begin.

With no nails and limited tools available, wood was lashed together with rope that was knotted and wrapped in a special way. My elder brother Michael (called *Odu*) and I were eager to learn how. I tied and wrapped with great care, imitating my Father's experienced style.

"Is this the right way?" I asked. I was anxious to be helpful, but another lesson was on its way.

Father scrutinized my rope work with care. Finally, he shook his head. "You must follow the method I teach you," he said. "If you do not, the house will collapse."

Patiently, he demonstrated the proper lashing technique again, until I was able to master it.

As the wooden frame progressed, we prepared an adhesive for the walls of the house, using mud and herbs to form a sticky plaster. Soon, a sturdy frame house was standing. The last part of home building involved raising the roof. This was a crucial process for the integrity of the house, and we were careful to weave tight mats of bamboo to keep the weather out.

While our home was being built, my parents did not neglect the planting of food. When my father had said the land near Ambuluwa Mountain was unspoiled, he was understating the truth. The land was so fertile that plants seemed to spring to life wherever seed touched earth. When we first moved into the wilderness, we had nothing but some provisions that we had carried from my uncle's village. It wasn't long, though, before we were truly self-sufficient. I can't remember a time when we didn't have plenty of fresh, delicious food provided for us from God's bounty.

We drank from running streams. There was no pollution. Birds and animals of all kinds, such as ostriches, giraffes, leopards, elephants, buffalo, and many others inhabited the forest. The work was very hard, but the land rewarded our efforts lavishly.

We were a happy family. Though we were refugees driven from our true homeland by war, we did not live as oppressed people. My parents protected us from that. We just knew that we were temporarily living in another land. My parents would often talk about going home to southern Sudan someday.

## Putting Down Stakes

By the time we were settled in our wilderness home, all of our relatives were scattered throughout Uganda. My maternal grandfather, Rabbi Vuni, left with his remaining family to settle in Gulu. We were unable to maintain contact with them during this time of political chaos, but we did find out later that Grandfather built and pastored a church in Gulu. He sent two of my uncles, Abednego and Niklaus, to study at a seminary in Nairobi, Kenya.

In the Ugandan wilderness, we knew nothing of going to church. But we came to realize that we were part of the body of Christ. My parents taught us about God and told us stories from the Bible. Our home was always open for fellowship and prayer. The great tamarind tree became a sort of outdoor chapel where we all would gather to sing and worship. We had no money, so we joyfully brought the firstfruits of all our labor as an offering to the Lord. In keeping with our Hebrew heritage, we never failed to remember the traditional feasts and holidays. We were so thankful for God's provision of a refuge for our family.

Soon, several Christian friends of ours from South Sudan began to hear of the little village that my father had started, and they came with their whole families to join us. Little by little, our tamarind tree covered a congregation. Over time, with many hands to help, the work of plowing fields and raising roofs became lighter. Eventually, we had a flourishing community with men to build silos and women to weed the gardens and children to grow up together.

We called our new village Ambuluwa. Our home was no longer a wilderness.

# Chapter 2

# Ambuluwa

AS OUR LITTLE village grew, our family continued to grow and prosper. My parents adopted a boy about my age named Francis. His mother was a relative in my father's family, but the child's father, a Ugandan trader, abandoned them both. Francis needed a stable family, and our family always had room for one more child. My little sister Rose was born, and she became a wonderful playmate and friend.

My older sisters, in the Levite tradition, were given responsibilities as women in our household. To me, they were surrogate mothers. They had full maternal authority over me, and I was obliged to obey them in everything. They carried me around on their backs through the day as they completed their chores. They cared for me and taught me, and I loved them very much.

My elder, Michael, was the oldest male child, and in our tradition, that meant that many hopes and expectations were invested in him. We called him "Odu," which means "give thanks to the Lord." When women marry, they leave the family to join the family of their new husbands; when men marry, they remain a part of their family of origin. So it was that Odu was sent to school as soon as it was possible to send him. My father knew that education would be the key to advancement of our people, and he hoped that Odu would succeed in this endeavor as a representative of our family.

All the other families in the community respected my father, the founder of our village. He was elected to positions of leadership whenever the need arose. He served as a judge or counselor in the resolution of disputes among neighbors. And both of my parents often advised other couples on issues related to family relationships. Their advice was respected because they lived godly lives; and their answers were thoughtful, fair, and always based on biblical principles.

In Ambuluwa, we never heard of anyone committing a crime, murdering someone, or abusing drugs and alcohol. There was no need for a prison. Although wild animals of every kind surrounded us, there were no guns. Our spears, arrows, and axes were for hunting or cutting wood. Anyone who purchased a gun was considered to be in error. In our minds, there was no purpose for a gun except to kill.

Family was the core of our society. It was considered shameful to be unmarried and without children. Children were considered a blessing of tremendous value. But divorce and children born out of wedlock were viewed as a stain on the entire family and a force of destruction in the community. For this reason, sexual immorality was absolutely prohibited. If a single girl became pregnant, she and her boyfriend would be given the opportunity to marry. If the boy refused, he would be publicly flogged and forced to pay a dowry price. Then he would forever forfeit the child that he had fathered to the girl and her family. He would be marked as unfit for marriage and would carry that shameful label for the rest of his life. Fortunately, this situation did not arise very often, and most marriages were arranged. The parents of a girl would take notice of a young man if he was hardworking, industrious, and of good moral character. This would be the type of man they would identify for their daughter to marry.

In the Levitical tradition, the groom had to pay a price for his bride. Then he would return to his parents' home to prepare a place for her. The period of preparation could take anywhere from six months to a year. When the new home was prepared, the bride's parents would invite the groom and his whole family to a banquet. After the wedding feast, the groom would return during the night to claim his bride.

Some Westerners may feel that paying a price for a bride is like purchasing a slave. This is not true. The relationships in the family are strong and loving, not at all demeaning or cruel. Women are equal partners in the Levitical home. The ancient tradition also echoes a beautiful scriptural illustration of

Christ and His church. Our Savior paid a price for us, and even now He is preparing a place for us in heaven. When He returns, He will claim us and we will live with Him forever. When I see all the pain and destruction in families today, it breaks my heart. I wish everyone could experience the love and security of families like those in our village.

## Around the O

When I was a child, we didn't have modern conveniences. There was no electricity, no telephone, no refrigerator, no TV, no radio, no movies. Even so, we did not want for entertainment during the evening hours. At the equator, we had twelve hours of daylight and twelve hours of night. This did not vary through the year. With no electricity, we found an inventive way to spend the hours before bedtime. Our entire community would gather together around the "O."

The O was a great circle that formed around a blazing fire. The fire was a place for fun, fellowship, and wonderful songs and stories (some more true than others). Everyone was given the chance to join in. It was a special time for everyone in the village, and it was a special job to be chosen to gather the firewood for the O. I remember the joy of going with my big brother to prepare the wood for the O.

Odu and I would hike through the underbrush, gathering dry sticks. The sun was already low on the horizon by that time, so we always needed to hurry. Wildlife became more active at dusk, so it was important to be out of the woods by nightfall.

On one of our gathering expeditions, I remember Odu suddenly freezing in his tracks. "William," he hissed, "look at this!"

I followed his gaze to an area near some bushes, and to my horror I saw a python squeezing the life out of a dog. "Let's pull the snake off of him," I whispered.

"Are you crazy? That python will constrict you if you try to grab him." Odu stood silent for a moment, frowning in concentration. "I know," he said at last. "Come on, let's get some arrows."

My brother and I turned and ran back to the village. Odu grabbed his bow and arrow and we raced back to the forest. Could we get back in time to save the dog?

The dog was still alive when we returned. Odu loaded his arrow and drew his bow. The arrow flew straight into the snake's head. As the python expired, his coils relaxed, and we were able to release the dog. The dog looked up at us with gratitude, but the animal was having difficulty drawing breath. The snake had crushed his ribs.

"It's too late." Odu stooped to stroke the dying dog's matted fur. "He can't breathe."

We stayed and watched as the dog died, feeling sad and helpless. Then we turned back toward the village. It was nearly time for the O, and we needed to finish gathering firewood. The stories would help to cheer us up.

There was a proverb in our village: "Don't believe everything you hear around the O!" Sometimes the rumors and gossip would fly. Of course, even as children we knew that some things were best not spoken of in public. Most of the time, people spoke of history, of legend, of politics, or just plain fiction. It was all in fun.

Many of the stories used animals as characters; and since we all knew it was only a tall tale, the storyteller could let his imagination run wild. Sometimes the stories were hilarious and outrageous, and sometimes quite scary. But around the fire, we all felt safe. When the fables and folktales began to wind down, we often spoke of spiritual things. It was a time to pray and sing worship songs together.

On clear nights, the skies would literally light up with a vast expanse of sparkling stars. When the moon was full, the light would be eerily bright, casting faint shadows through the trees and homes of our village. Nighttime in Ambuluwa was so deep and immense that it was natural to ask the Creator, "What is man, that thou art mindful of him?"

## In the Dark of the Night

But for all its beauty, night also brought danger to the village. I remember one night when we had all been sitting around the O for some time. My paternal grandfather, Karan Levi, had been telling one of his funny stories but was now ready to head back to his house and turn in for the night. Grandpa Levi was blind, and his once-handsome face was scarred. His eyes had been put out during a beating that he had received as a young man at the hands of some Muslims who hadn't approved of his religion and ethnicity. He wasn't bitter about it, but sometimes he could be hard on a little kid like me. He needed to be led about whenever he wanted to go somewhere, and I was often the one who had to lead him. If I didn't come to him quickly enough, I would get in trouble.

"Eh, Dark Neck!" the old man called. "Take me home."

Grandpa always called me "Long Neck" or "Dark Neck" as a sort of nickname.

"Ahh, I wanted to hear another story," I whined.

Even from across the bonfire, I could see my mother's withering gaze. She didn't need to say a word. With a sigh, I got up and scampered over to Grandfather.

"C'mon, Francis, help me bring some firewood for Grandpa and Grandma." I nudged my adopted brother, who got up to accompany me. We picked up some wood that was still warm from the fire to carry back for our grandparents.

"Here I am, Grandpa," I said, reaching out to hold his hand. He stood and nodded good night to the rest of the villagers. He was a tall man, still straight and strong. It was a shame that he was unable to see.

Without electricity in our homes, those of us with sight had no advantage over the blind at nighttime. Away from the light of the fire and the glow of the stars, it was pitch-black inside my grandparents' house. I literally could not see my hand in front of my face. Francis and I helped our grandparents inside, and then I brought an armload of warm wood in for the hearth.

Suddenly, I stopped still as death. I could feel the hairs on the back of my neck prickle with foreboding. I had the sensation that someone or something was watching me from the darkness—something bad.

At that moment, a horrible rushing sound came toward me. I dropped the glowing wood, scattering stinging embers at my feet. I heard myself scream as I turned and ran. Francis was outside the door, and he heard my screams. We both ran back to the O as fast as we possibly could.

"Abba! Help!" I panted. I was trembling with shock and fear. "Something terrible is inside of Grandpa's house. You must help him."

I heard a few guffaws around the circle. The adults thought Francis and I were making up a good story.

"You are just saying that. Don't make up stories," Father said.

"No, I am serious! There is something there—it tried to attack me. I don't know what it is. Please, come and see what it is."

Francis, wide-eyed, nodded in agreement. Murmurs arose, and most of the grown-ups quickly got up to go to Grandpa's house, carrying torches to light the way.

When the flames illuminated Grandpa's small house, we discovered what it was that had nearly gotten ahold of me—a fifteen-foot-long python!

"Wow, the kids were telling the truth," someone said. "They could have been squeezed to death."

"It must have been looking for a warm spot," remarked Father.

Everyone knew that a large python was serious business. In the darkness, it could have killed either of my grandparents that night. The adults debated among themselves how best to destroy the snake. They consulted the man who was considered the most knowledgeable about snake killing.

"Well," he said slowly, "we have to go for the head if we don't want anyone to get hurt." He directed a group of men to grab the head of the snake at his signal. "I'll cut off his head as quick as I can."

The men swiftly executed their plan, and the snake was slain. I couldn't help thinking about the dog I had seen dying in the coils of a python not long before. I shuddered with the knowledge that Grandfather, Grandmother, Francis, and I had come so close to being python prey. God had protected us once again.

## A Good Childhood

As a child, I grew up depending completely on God to take care of me. Snakes, illnesses, and natural disasters were always a possibility in our lives, but we did not fear. Neither were we concerned about the provision of food, shelter, or clothing. We trusted that God would supply everything we needed. As we lived in harmony with God's creation, His provision was obvious to us all.

My family and my village combined our Christian faith with our rich Hebrew heritage as we lived in the wilderness. Everything was under God's control. Western countries would likely regard our little

village of Ambuluwa as "backward" and "impover-
ished." But now that I have seen both ways of life, I
wonder who it is that really lives in poverty. In
Ambuluwa, we were rich in love, community, and
faith. All in all, it was a pretty good way to grow
up.

# Chapter 3

# Little Shepherds

IN OUR TINY community of Ambuluwa, it took the efforts of all the little children to cause the village to thrive. Every person, no matter how small, had a duty to do his or her very best for the well-being of their parents, brothers, sisters, and neighbors. Nobody was given a free ride—everybody had to do the share of work for which each one was best suited.

The task of shepherding generally fell to the youngest boys. Although the work was not physically strenuous, it could be dangerous, and it entailed a great deal of responsibility. I began shepherding at age five. I was just a skinny slip of a boy, weighing no more than forty pounds. I was proud to be given such an important job.

I remember the day when my brother Francis and I were introduced to our special role. We were busy doing the work reserved for babies—frightening birds.

"Gimme that rock, Francis!" I yelled, wresting the small gray projectile from his hand. I ran straight toward a tree with branches that dipped gracefully down over a patch of Mother's best maize. I had spotted a group of hungry birds swooping down from the sheltering boughs like kamikaze fighters, expert in the art of "seek and destroy." I was not eager to share my family's dinner with thieves. Running as fast as my small legs would carry me, I heaved the rock at the branches.

"Shoo, birds, go away!"

The birds were spooked briefly, and they fluttered up to higher branches, eyeing Francis and me with cocked heads and beady eyes. I guess they were sizing us up, because it didn't take long for them to decide that we weren't too frightening. Certainly, we weren't enough of a threat to keep them at bay for more than a few seconds. It was just a minor inconvenience to the flock of feathered diners to see two human children leaping in the air and making silly human noises. They were confident that we would eventually tire of the activity, and they were right. Before long, we were out of breath and had to stop hopping.

We were looking around for a more promising activity when Father summoned us.

He was hard at work as usual, pounding stakes into the ground and wrapping them together into some sort of tightly woven structure. He straightened up for a moment when we approached.

"Boys," Father said as he wiped sweat from his forehead with a dusty hand, "I have a job for you to do."

We stood attentively, waiting for orders while our dad turned back to his work. A man as hardworking as Father knew how to talk and work at the same time when something important needed to be done.

"Hold this here while I drive it into the ground."

He hit a tough wooden stake until it was buried deeply in the soil. The stakes formed slats that were placed closely together, forming a strong wall.

"What are we building?" Francis asked.

"This will be a new stable for the sheep and goats." Father grabbed another slat and nodded at Francis, who quickly held it in place. "That's what I wanted to talk to you boys about."

We waited as he pounded the wood deeply into the soil.

"You know, now that Michael is away at school, I need someone to take care of the animals. William. Francis. It's time for you to learn how to be shepherds. The first thing you are going to learn is how to build a pen. You help me, and you will learn how to do it next time."

As he spoke, he lashed the wood together tightly, forming a strong stockade.

"Why do you have to put them so close together?" I said. "The sheep are way too big to fit between that."

"Because this pen isn't to keep the sheep in as much as it is to keep the hyenas out."

"Hyenas?" I had heard scary stories about these vicious carnivores, and it made me a little nervous to think about hyenas stalking our sheep.

"You have to be careful; those hyenas will rip a sheep open and eat it alive. They suck out the intestines and leave the carcass."

I didn't reply. The mental image of a hyena ripping open our sheep, which I loved almost as if they were pets, was unsettling. I looked over at Francis. He looked scared.

Father continued. "You have to drive the stakes in deep too, because those hyenas will dig a hole right under a shallow-driven fence. And even though they only eat one sheep, they won't stop killing until they've killed several."

"That doesn't make any sense," I said. We hunted wild animals, but we never killed for sport. We only killed for the purpose of feeding our family. The thought of a wild animal killing other animals for no reason was foreign to me.

"You're right. It doesn't make sense." He stood up again, bending backwards a bit to stretch his sore muscles. "That's why it's your job to watch out for hyenas, and other wild animals, to protect the sheep. You have to be especially careful when you drive the sheep near caves, because that's where all sorts of predators like to hang out, waiting for dinner. If you see one, stand up on a rock and shout to scare it away. Don't lead the sheep near the bushes in the evenings, because a python might grab one. And make sure the sheep don't step on any of the poisonous snakes. You have to keep a sharp eye out for them."

Francis and I stood proudly, like soldiers being commissioned into honorable service. "We will do our best," I said.

Now that I live in the United States, I realize that modern parents consider children to be fragile creatures, incapable of assuming responsibility or of facing danger. In retrospect, I'm sure my parents were concerned about my safety, but in our community we relied on God to protect us—and our way of life had flourished for as long as anyone could recall.

Mom and Dad were diligent to instruct us about how to deal with any possible danger. For example, they told us how to survive in a stampede of wild buffalo by lying flat on the ground. They explained why it would be a mistake to keep on running, because the animals would sweep us up with their horns, and we would be gored and trampled to death. My father also was careful to explain how to keep watch for poisonous snakes and constrictors. Although the constrictors—such as the pythons—were not venomous, they could ambush and crush a child or a sheep in tight, muscular coils.

Since my father could not swim, he was particularly concerned about the rivers. He warned us that we could easily be swept away in the headwaters, fast-flowing streams that fed water from the mountains down into the great Nile River. We listened carefully to his instructions and committed everything to memory.

## Adventures in Shepherding

When we began our shepherding duties, we soon discovered that working in the forest wasn't always difficult or scary. It could be fun!

The forest was filled with tempting activities for a small boy, and I admit that there were times when the sheep did not receive the attention that they deserved. I loved to climb trees and swing from vines in the thick jungle foliage. Since I was so light, I was a great climber. Francis and I enjoyed making swing sets by tying bits of wood between vines and hanging them several feet from the jungle floor, almost like a trapeze. Of course, sometimes they would break and I suffered some terrible falls. But God protected me from serious injury. We also made see-saws from wood that we wedged into the crook of a tree. It was fun to balance with Francis as we teetered up and down.

Another tree produced giant fibrous pods that we used to cut off and hollow out into a sort of canoe that was big enough to sit in. Then we would carve out a U-shaped trail in a muddy riverbank and ride the canoe down the hill into the water. We couldn't have found a better ride in any amusement park.

While we were caring for the animals, we lived off the land. We never had to pack our lunch when we brought our herds out to graze. We made rubber slingshots out of an elastic resin and used them to shoot birds to eat. The forest held a vast bounty of tropical fruits as well. They were fresh, sweet, and delicious, as well as a good source of vitamins. We drank water from clear, clean streams, and caught fresh fish. We were never hungry. There was even a special type of tree that was used for cleaning our teeth.

I have fond memories of days spent having fun in the jungle. Unfortunately, there were days when I had too much fun. On one of those days, while I was enjoying a homemade swing, my mind began to wander. As if on cue, my sheep and goats began to wander too—right into a neighbor's field. That day, they enjoyed a choice meal of beans and cassava.

"William!" From the sound of my father's voice, I knew I was in big trouble. Father could see me swinging from the tree. There was nothing I could do but climb down and face my punishment.

"You let the sheep get into our neighbor's field. They have destroyed a large area of the crop. What do you have to say for yourself?"

I hung my head in shame. The crop was the lifeblood of our village; we needed the harvest to survive. The value of produce was like currency to us, because we did not have money for trade. Crop damage was very serious.

"I'm sorry," I said through my tears, but I couldn't bring myself to look up.

"Our neighbor was furious. You will have to be punished for this, and I must make restitution for the damage you caused."

I didn't always respond well to discipline, but my parents believed that to spare the rod was to spoil the child. They always made it very clear that I was expected to obey. Obedience in the wilderness was not just a matter of being a well-behaved little boy. It was literally a matter of life and death. That is why God tells us in the Ten Commandments that we ought to honor our father and our mother that our days may be long in the land that the Lord has given us. I can think of several instances when my disobedience in failing to heed my parents' instructions almost led to my death. But I learned from my mistakes, and most of the time I did what I was instructed to do.

## Reading the Seasons

Time passed quickly, and I began to understand more and more about the cycles of life and the seasons in the forest. I learned to live in harmony with the natural world around me, and I sensed God's design and purpose in everything. Even events that on the surface seemed disastrous were all a part of His plan for the renewal and sustenance of His creation.

Uganda lies on the earth's equator and, consequently, has a very unique climate. There is no summer or winter on the equator; it's just the rainy season and the dry season. Both had the potential to produce hazardous conditions for shepherds. I remember vividly a terrifying day in late June when I was seven, at the end of a long dry season.

"Ouch, I stepped on another thorn," Francis said as he bent over to pull a long spine from the sole of his foot. He massaged it gingerly until a single drop of blood was expressed, then tossed the offending stem into the bushes.

"That's nothing," I said. "I've been stepping on those things all day. You don't see me complaining about it."

"I hate the dry season. Do you think we're in for a big drought?"

"Naw," I answered. "I heard Grandpa say that it was just about time for the rains to come, and he's always right about that sort of thing."

"I sure hope so," added Francis. "The grass couldn't get much drier than this. And it's so hot out here."

We stopped in a clearing that had plenty of grass for our herds to graze. The sheep and goats seemed content to munch on the stuff that by this time of year had the consistency of straw.

Francis and I found a shady spot and picked some fruit to eat. We were already feeling tired and hungry, though it was only midday. Perhaps we should have noticed the change in the way the birds chattered and screeched, but we didn't. We just rested and enjoyed our fruit.

"William," Francis whispered, "what's bothering the animals? Do you think there is a predator nearby?" He pointed silently to one of the goats. The creature anxiously pawed the ground while lifting his head up high to sniff the air. The other animals had stopped grazing and appeared uneasy.

I jumped to my feet, my heart thudding with a sudden rush of adrenaline. Francis was right—the animals were acting strangely. I grabbed my spear and turned slowly, scanning the bushes and trees.

Was something out there, stalking the sheep? I was afraid it might be a pack of wild dogs or hyenas.

Suddenly, the underbrush shook and several small animals virtually exploded into the clearing. They were all running away—from something.

"Francis, what is going on? I don't like this at all!"

"Me neither. Let's go home!"

Getting the herd together was not easy. The spooked animals weren't obeying our directions. Francis and I ran and shouted, gathering the sheep and goats as well as we could. Wild animals continued to crash through the underbrush, oblivious to our presence. The air, which had only recently been hot and still, was now rushing past our ears with a great whooshing sound. A thunderous roar was approaching our little clearing with horrifying speed and intensity. There was no longer any doubt about the nature of the threat that the animals had sensed.

"Fire!" Francis looked at me, his eyes widened with terror.

"We have to get the animals out of here! Run!"

The animals needed no more prodding. They were panicked, running away from the raging flames that consumed more and more of the tinder-dry forest each instant. Cinders flew everywhere, igniting new patches of brown grass and parched underbrush. We no longer felt the pain of razor-sharp thorns as they tore at our legs and feet. Our eyes burned from desiccated air and smoke, and our lungs ached with each breath. We were all running for our lives.

"Over here! Boys, come this way!"

Soon we could hear the shouts of the men from the village. They had seen the smoke, and they knew that we would need help. There were shepherd boys from each family wandering as far as four to five miles from safety. Everyone from the village was there to help gather boys and sheep and to protect Ambuluwa itself.

Finally we were safe behind a strip of scorched earth. The fire could only burn through once, so we were out of danger.

When the threat to the village had passed, I was surprised to see a group of men gather with spears and arrows to chase the forest fire. They seemed to be in high spirits. I clung to my mother, still shell-shocked from my encounter with one of the most powerful forces in nature. I didn't understand why some men wanted to go back toward the fire.

"Mama," I whispered, pulling on her dress, "why are they all going back to the fire?"

"All the animals of the forest will run out ahead of the fire," she replied. "It will be an easy hunt for them." She squeezed my shoulders in a gentle hug. "But you can stay here with me."

I was more than happy to oblige. To this day, that forest fire remains as one of the most frightening experiences in my life.

Not long after the fire swept through the forest, the rainy season arrived—right on schedule. Within days, fresh green shoots began to appear through the ashes in a vigorous burst of renewal.

Grandpa Levi explained to me that the destruction of the forest was not really destruction at all, but a new beginning. Just as God brings trials into the lives of His children to create change and growth, He brings the cycle of drought, fire, and rain to create fresh growth and new life on the earth. And soon the rainy season brought violent conditions of its own—sudden thunderstorms and raging torrents where once there were peaceful streams.

Each time Francis and I encountered some new danger, we grew in knowledge and confidence. Fires, floods, snakes, and predators were just part of growing up as a shepherd boy in Uganda. Although we gained confidence in our abilities, we never got cocky or too sure of ourselves. We were all too aware of the powerful and capricious forces of nature that we had to contend with. Only God could protect us from His creation, because He is the One whom the wind and the waves and the beasts obey.

I learned so many things from my job tending the sheep—the value of hard work, the importance of responsibility, and the necessity of obedience. I saw the beauty of God's natural world and learned how to respect it and care for it. But most of all, I gained a deep understanding of my Savior's love for me.

Even so, I was getting older—almost eight years old. And I began to long for the chance to learn how to read and write. I wished that I could go to school.

*Chapter 4*

# New
# Friends

IN EARLY 1972, I could hardly contain my excitement. *I was going to go to school!* The Catholic
church had opened up an elementary school for
refugee children, and I had a chance to attend. I was
bursting with the kind of wild energy that eight-
year-olds possess in abundance. My arms and legs
took on a fidgety life of their own as Mother and
Father discussed my fate. I dared to hope—I dared
to feel *sure* that they would let Francis and me go.

The primary schools would no longer admit children once they reached a certain age. At around
eleven years old, any refugee child who had not yet
begun his schooling would have to abandon all hope
of an education. Older children without any literacy
skills simply remained at home in their family
groups and learned the trade of their fathers. I loved

my parents, and I loved farming the rich earth; but I could not bear the thought of being left out of the world of the future.

There was a problem that would have to be overcome, however, and it was quite pressing. If Francis and I were to attend school during the day, there would be no one to take care of the flock. My parents were too busy farming to take on the extra job of herding the livestock. Neither one of them had ever had the opportunity to attend school, but they understood the importance of a good education, especially in a world that they saw changing before their very eyes in so many ways. Deep down, they knew the way of life they had enjoyed for so many generations was threatened, and they were determined to make sure their children were prepared for whatever the future would bring. But even so, there was a more immediate dilemma—who would shepherd the sheep? I tried not to listen as my parents debated the issue in hushed but urgent tones.

"Don't worry yourself, Ajjugo," my grandfather said loudly enough to be heard above the discussion that my parents were engaged in. "I will shepherd the sheep in William's place."

My parents exchanged glances, and for a moment their deliberation was stilled. "Father . . ." My father paused awkwardly as he struggled to frame a gentle response.

Grandpa Levi waved his hands dismissively. "I know, I know—I'm a blind old man. But that doesn't mean I don't know a thing or two about shepherding. Maybe even more than you, Son."

My father took the bait. "Okay, I'm listening."

"We will drive stakes into the field, one for each sheep. I will tie each sheep to a tether, and the sheep can graze as much as they want without wandering away. When they have eaten all the grass within their reach, we can place the stakes in fresh pasture."

Grandfather leaned toward me, and his leathery hands traced the shape of my face and neck. He smiled warmly at me, causing the scars on his face to twist happily. "Little Long Neck here will finally be able to go to school. He's a good boy."

"Thank you, Grandpa!" I wrapped my small arms around his frame in a grateful hug. I knew that he was making a sacrifice for me, and I would not forget it.

Mother chuckled softly, and then I knew the issue was settled. "So, William," she teased, "you are a good boy, are you? Now you have to be a smart boy too."

"Yes, Mama!" I exclaimed. "I *am* smart, you'll see!"

"I guess this means you boys will be needing some supplies." Father's statement was meant as a nod of approval to Grandfather's plan. He leaned back and pressed his hands together, like he always did when he was thinking hard about something.

It was no small thing in those days to find school supplies. We couldn't just stop by the local discount mart and stock up on pencils, papers, and notebooks. And for the first time in my life, I was acutely aware that I had never owned a pair of shoes. The soles of my feet were as tough and leathery as a buffalo hide from the thorns, hot embers, and sharp stones that had etched their legacy into my unprotected skin. Shoes would be nice, but I knew I didn't really need them to make the trip to school. I would need a book bag and something to write with. That was the bare minimum.

I looked up, and I could tell that the wheels were still turning in my father's head. I wondered what he was planning. Soon, I had my answer.

The next day, I woke up to find that Father had loaded up a bundle of freshly harvested cotton and was filling some jars with water. He was getting ready to go somewhere.

"Come on, boys," he boomed, waving Francis and me over to his side. "We're going to get some school supplies."

I had never been to a town before, and I had never seen a store. The thought of going on a trip to buy school supplies was as exotic to me as a voyage to the moon. I was ready to go immediately, but Abba had other plans. "Anna," he called to my mama, "bring out Michael and the girls."

Soon our whole family was gathered around the big bundles of cotton. My father held my mother's hand and bowed his head.

"Dear heavenly Father," he prayed, "we dedicate this, the firstfruits of our cotton harvest, to You. As we send the boys to school, we pray that You will use this cotton to grow these children into educated men in Your service. Lord, we dedicate this cotton to You, and we dedicate these boys to You also. Amen."

I opened my eyes and scanned the faces of the members of my dear family. Everyone was looking at Francis and me, and I was filled with gratitude at the knowledge of their sacrifice on our behalf. It was sobering to think of myself as a grown-up some-day, serving God with an education purchased with a load of cotton.

The ten-mile walk to a neighboring village seemed to take no time at all. The town was called Wili-Wili, and Sudanese refugees populated it. Some of the people who lived there had been merchants and craftsmen back in the old country, and they had set up a market with real shops and many wonderful products. I took in the sights with a sense of awe. The first shop we entered was that of a tailor. Father approached the owner of the establishment with a sample of our fine cotton.

"Yes, it is fine, healthy-looking cotton," the man remarked. He reached out to accept a piece from my father. He pulled at the strands carefully and smoothed them between his narrow fingers. "What do you need?"

Father pointed to some bolts of material that were stored against the wall. "We need short-sleeved shirts from the green cloth, and I'll take some of the khaki to make into backpacks."

The tailor smiled and nodded toward Francis and me. "Boys going to school?"

"Yes, sir," my father replied with a broad grin. His muscular frame straightened with pride. "These boys are sharp."

"We need boys like that," the tailor said. There

was a serious note in his voice that let me know his was more than a casual remark to humor children. I remembered the prayer my father had offered that morning on our behalf, and for a moment I felt the gravity of the hope that was being invested in me. I knew deep down that the future of our people would depend on little boys like Francis and me.

## School Is In

I'll never forget my first day at school. The hardest part was the commute. We had to walk several miles to the neighboring town of Nyigeri. It was a small town but near the dirt road that led from Uganda to Sudan. Although no one had a car, the town of Nyigeri was accessible by virtue of that little road, and that made it an important location.

School started at eight o'clock sharp. We didn't have clocks, so we got up with the crowing of the cock just before dawn. We figured that six o'clock was about the time of sunrise, and we knew that it would take at least two hours to walk to school if we kept a brisk pace and the rivers were running low. There weren't any roads, but enough people traveled between villages to form a beaten trail. The trail passed over four rivers, and during rainy season these rivers became raging torrents, making the walk to school treacherous. Sometimes we would get drenched or lose our books in the water. In the dry season, the savannah grass was so tall that it became difficult to pass. Thankfully, my first days of school were in January, and the trail was not too tough to travel then.

It was great running to school with my big brother, Michael, who by then was in the highest grade in the school, primary three. Francis and I were going to be starting primary one.

The facilities consisted of two large mud buildings with thatch roofs. Catholics ran the school, which explained the prayers before classes and the Bible lessons in religion class. Of course, we also had lessons in health and hygiene, English, and reading and writing. Most of the teaching was done in our tribal language, Madi. I loved learning the alphabet.

We learned many songs in school, but I remember one song in particular helped motivate us to study. Our headmaster required us to sing this song each day. It was sung in Madi, but its meaning was something like this:

> *I want to know the alphabet, so that when I*
>   *grow up*
> *And I have an education; I will know how to*
>   *read and how to write.*
> *I can go into foreign countries.*
> *I can speak other languages. I can speak in English.*
> *I will speak correctly so people can understand me.*
> *And when I come back to my country, I will*
>   *develop my country.*
> *I will also raise the people's standard of living.*

Our headmaster was a mentor to us, and he was trying to prepare us mentally for the long struggle to reclaim our own country. Like other adults, he considered us a precious resource for the future.

Our teachers were all refugees, just like us, and we loved them for what they were doing for us. We all held steadfastly to the things that gave us hope—God, family, and education.

After the morning lesson, it was time to break for recess. We all rushed outside, excited to be able to play with kids our own age. One boy in my class wasn't from my village, but I had seen him before. His name was Michael Longwa. He was a relative of my mother's family, and his mom was a widow. His dad, Mama's cousin, had been a chaplain in the Anya-Nya army. Jihad forces had killed him when Michael was too young to remember.

"Hi, William! Hi, Francis!" Michael ambled over to us with a sneaky look on his face. "Want to play some soccer?"

Michael Longwa was about my size, but he had a reputation for being tough. I hoped his invitation to play soccer wasn't an invitation to get flattened.

"Sure," Francis answered without hesitation. "Let's set up some goals."

As Francis and some other boys gathered long sticks to use as goalposts, Michael approached me and produced his soccer ball. It was nothing but a ball of old clothes tied together with strings, but Michael tossed it like it was regulation.

"Betcha can't beat me," Michael teased coolly.

I reached out to grab the ball, but Michael stepped aside, throwing me off balance.

"It's all in the footwork, William," Michael

snickered as I stumbled forward. "Who wants to be on my team?" he called.

We played soccer every day at recess. It was the most fun any of us could remember. Michael was very competitive, and I thought he was a real show-off. Even so, we became friends. He was also competitive with schoolwork, and I was glad to have him as a study partner.

Lunchtime was another break from the work of the day. We liked to go out and look at the road that ran through Nyigeri.

"I heard that sometimes cars come through this way," Michael said. He kicked at the gravel lining the edge of the packed dirt, sending up a little puff of dust.

"I would love to see a car!" I said.

"Someday, I'm gonna *drive* one," Michael Longwa shot back, eager to top me in even our daydreaming moments.

My older brother came up behind us. "You kids haven't seen anything yet," he bragged. "I saw a jeep from the Ugandan army drive through here before."

"Aw, that must have been great," I said enviously. After that, I made a mental note to keep an eye on the road, just in case.

Francis and I were exhausted at the end of every school day, and it took some time for us to adjust to the rigors of our new routine. At times we thought it would be easier to go back to shepherding, but then we would remember how blessed we were to be receiving an education. Father's bartered gift of cotton would someday bear fruit for the Lord.

# Chapter 5

# The Addis Ababa Agreement

THE NEWS SPREAD like brush fire in the dry season. The air crackled with excitement and the sound of grown-ups talking together. I didn't quite understand the importance of what was about to happen, but I knew I was about to go on an adventure with my whole family. In fact, all of the families in the village would be going on this adventure to Chinyaquia, a small city on the border of Uganda and Sudan where there was to be a ceremony commemorating the peace treaty that had been reached between northern and southern Sudan. Could the civil war finally be over?

My father looked serious, and he was speaking rapidly to my mother, his hands accenting each syllable. "I don't trust them, Anna," he said, striking the palm of his hand down on a table emphatically.

"Even when the British left in 1956, I knew deep down that they would plot against our people. There can never be unity between the North and the South—can the leopard change his spots?"

"Ajjugo." My mother placed her hand gently on Father's arm. "Can't we dare to feel hope for our people? Just for a little while?"

Father drew Mother close for a moment, as if to gain strength from her nearness. "I really want to—you *know* I do."

"Then hope," Mother said. "But hope in the Lord. Just like it says in the Bible, there are some who trust in chariots, and some in horses; but we will remember the name of the Lord our God."

A trace of a smile softened Father's expression. "I knew there was a reason I married the preacher's daughter." He paused for a moment. "Thank God we have something more than politics to give us hope. I have to tell you, Anna, as much as I agree—well, I just can't. There's too much history telling me otherwise."

Now it was Mother's turn to look serious. "So what are we going to do, Ajjugo? What will this mean for the children?"

Father looked around to see several sets of eyes fixed upon him. He took it as his cue to change the subject. "What are we going to do?" He straightened his shoulders and grinned broadly. "Why, Anna, we're going to Chinyaquia, of course!"

## Planes, Jeeps, and Kuro

The whole village was buzzing about the trip to Chinyaquia. Every Sudanese in exile who was able to make the journey was certain to be there. People were singing and smiling, like they were going to a wedding party or a festival instead of some political ceremony. The mood was contagious, and I soon forgot my father's misgivings.

"Hey, Michael," I called, running to greet my school friend. "I heard there will be airplanes!"

Michael Longwa's mother had brought him to visit, and she stood nearby, talking with my mother.

"Rrrrrrrrr!" Michael grabbed a toy car that he had made out of dried mud, sweeping it in a dramatic arc through the air. "There's gonna be jeeps too! And trucks!"

"This is going to be really fun," I said.

An older boy overheard us and leaned toward us. "There's gonna be *kuro* there too," he smirked. "And you know what they do to little kids like you." He chuckled to himself as he sauntered away.

"Don't listen to him, William," Michael said. "He's just trying to scare us."

*Kuro* was one of the names that the Madi people had for Arabs. They were also called *more* or *kuturia*. The Arab people were mysterious to us. We didn't understand the way they thought or the reasons for their actions. I had never seen an Arab before, but I had heard lots of stories—and they were scary. There were tales handed down about the children who were stolen away and sold to slave traders in India, the Middle East, and the Americas. Even Muhammad the prophet had owned slaves, so the Muslim people accepted slavery. The attacks by the Islamic military regime from Khartoum were fresh in our minds, as well. So the thought of actually seeing a kuro was a little frightening for a kid like me.

"I'm not scared," I told Michael. "My dad will protect us. And, besides, this is a peace agreement."

Michael nodded. "I'm not scared, either. I'm going to have *fun!*"

He punctuated the word "fun" by launching an airplane made of mud and straw into the air like a rocket. We both fell down laughing. It was going to be a great trip.

## "Are We There Yet?"

Our families were soon ready for the long trek to Chinyaquia. The Ugandan military had an outpost there, and there was a small airstrip too. Idi Amin Dada, the president of Uganda since a coup d'état the year before, had agreed to host a meeting between Jaafar Mohammed Nimieri, an Arab leader from Khartoum, and Joseph Lagu, an African leader representing South Sudan. Michael and I couldn't wait to see all the soldiers and important people.

"Are we almost there, Father?" I asked.

"Only about ten more miles," he replied gruffly.

My feet were getting swollen from walking so far without shoes.

"Just be glad you don't have to carry your little

brother," Mama chided. She handed me some fruit to quiet my grumbling.

Soon we were able to see Chinyaquia in the distance. A small airplane zipped across the sky! I watched, entranced, as the little craft circled and descended for a landing at the small white ribbon of an airstrip. In my excitement, I had forgotten all about my sore feet.

As we drew closer, my brother Michael pointed a finger at a dark line near the horizon. "Jeeps! Look at all the jeeps!"

It was true. There were hundreds of military vehicles crossing the border from Sudan. The Islamic military was using German-made trucks. They were painted green and filled with Arabs.

"Look at all the kuro, Mama!" I shouted. "They're our enemies!"

Mother was quick to correct me. "Our *enemy* is Satan. Jesus died for all of those Arabs just like He died for you and me. The Bible tells us that we must love the Arabs and pray for them too. Right, Ajjugo?"

Father's eyes met mine. His expression was stern. "Your mother is right. I don't want to hear you talking that way. I know you have heard me say that I don't trust these people. The Bible never said I needed to *trust* anybody—but it does say that it's wrong to speak evil of somebody made in God's image."

I felt my face flush. "I'm sorry," I mumbled.

As we approached the town, we realized that it was packed shoulder to shoulder with refugees. The people from our village were jostling for a place near the podium that had been set up for the ceremony.

The sun was white-hot, and the glare made me squint through the shimmering haze. I tried to jump up in the air to get a better view, but mostly what I saw was people—lots of hot, dusty people.

Idi Amin Dada had mobilized all the refugees within walking distance of the border town to witness an agreement. The agreement, signed in Addis Ababa, Ethiopia, was supposed to grant political autonomy to the Africans of southern Sudan. The civil war had reached an impasse, and the Khartoum government was tired of trying to put down the rebels. At the moment, it seemed to be in their best interest to make some sort of concession. All of the Sudanese refugees cherished the possibility that this might mean that they could return to the homes that they had longed to see for so many years.

"There's Idi Amin!" I heard people murmur in the crowd around me. I looked up and saw a large African man in full military dress. The Ugandan military men who accompanied him wore fatigues and carried rifles.

Soon after Mr. Amin ascended the platform, Joseph Lagu and Jaafar Mohammed Nimieri arrived, smiling and waving to the crowd. They were also dressed in military fatigues, and although they were opponents, they certainly seemed to be friendly enough.

"I heard Nimieri didn't even sign at Addis Ababa," a man in the crowd whispered to my father.

"True enough," Father replied. "Another negotiator signed in his place."

"That doesn't seem like a very good sign. An

agreement of convenience will be broken when it no longer serves the interests of Khartoum."

Father nodded slowly. "We have seen that before. . . ."

The conversation was cut short by cheers from the excited crowd. With great fanfare, Lagu and Nimieri were preparing to cut a red ribbon, a symbol of the opening of southern Sudan to her returning people. As the fragments of the delicate ribbon fluttered to the ground, a great roar erupted. It was an emotional moment for everyone. Under the new agreement, southern Sudan would have the authority to govern her own affairs without interference from the North. For millions of Sudanese refugees, it was a chance to go home at long last.

A throng of people pushed their way to the border. Parents hoisted young children up on shoulders to see, often for the first time, their homeland. I felt the pull of home on my heart at that moment as well. Even though I never thought of myself as a "refugee," I always knew that someday I would return to my real home. Just like my headmaster at the Nyigeri school had said, I knew that it would be up to me to do my part to rebuild Sudan.

I looked up at my father as he drank in the sight before us. I wondered what he was thinking. Then the muscle in his jaw tightened, and he turned around briskly. "Time to go," he said simply.

While others in the group that had traveled from our village talked excitedly amongst themselves, my dad remained silent. Mom didn't say anything to him; she just walked by his side. I figured she knew what he was thinking, as she usually did. What I didn't know was how much our lives were about to change.

That evening, back in Ambuluwa, we were all thoroughly exhausted. My feet were cracked and bleeding. Even so, there was so much excitement that I didn't want to sleep. My oldest sisters, Angela and Jemima, were lost in animated conversation. They had formed a little circle together with their boyfriends; occasionally one or the other of them would run over and say something to our parents. Even from where I was sitting, I could see how much they were smiling. I thought my sisters looked especially pretty when they smiled like that.

In fact, it seemed that the only people in the village who were not enthusiastic were my parents. My father, in particular, was unusually quiet.

Eventually, the adrenaline of the day's events gave way to heavy eyelids, and everyone finally settled into their homes for the night. I fell into a deep, dreamless sleep.

## Unexpected Exodus

It was mid-March in 1972, and I had only been in school at Nyigeri for a half-semester when the Addis Ababa Agreement took effect. I had just begun learning to read and write and making new friends. But the next day at school, I began to understand what was about to happen to our community and our school.

The headmaster gathered all of us together after

the morning prayers. He looked excited. "Children," he announced, "I have something important to tell you."

We listened attentively as our favorite teacher began to speak. "How many of you saw the ribbon-cutting ceremony at Chinyaquia?"

Every hand shot up.

"That's wonderful. Remember what you saw. It was a historic event! How many of you know what the Addis Ababa Agreement means?"

A few hands waved in the air, mostly from the primary three students. Even though I thought I understood what it meant, I wanted to hear what the headmaster had to say, so I kept my hand down.

The headmaster wiped his brow with a handkerchief. "What this agreement means is that the war is over," he said. "The government in Khartoum has agreed to allow all of us in the South to have a say in how we will be governed. That is certainly something to celebrate."

He cleared his throat and looked around at the student body. "I want to tell you all how much I have enjoyed teaching you." His voice faltered.

Francis elbowed me. "He looks like he is about to cry," he whispered.

"How many of you children will be leaving your villages?" the headmaster asked.

Again, hands shot up all over the group. Suddenly, I had a bad feeling in the pit of my stomach.

I elbowed Francis back. "Is everybody leaving?" I gasped. "What about us?"

Francis just looked at me and shrugged.

"I will be leaving as well," the headmaster continued. "Today will be my last day teaching at this school. May God bless all of you."

My head suddenly spun with the stark reality of our future. The students were leaving. The headmaster was leaving. *What will become of my school?*

That treaty had changed everything! No wonder my father had looked so serious. I wondered if we would be leaving Ambuluwa too. I wanted to go back to Sudan someday but not yet. I didn't know what to think.

During our lunch break, I sat down with Michael Longwa. We had become pretty good friends.

"So, William," Michael said between bites of lunch, "when is your family leaving?"

I didn't know what to say. "I'm not sure; my father hasn't told us yet." Actually, I knew the Levi family wasn't going anywhere soon.

"Mama and I are leaving tomorrow," Michael said casually. "We're going back to Moli Township, back to the old village."

"Tomorrow?" was all I could manage. "Oh."

"Mama told me that your family used to live not too far from us," Michael continued.

"Maybe we'll see each other again when we get there."

"Sure!" Michael got up and brushed the crumbs from his lap. "It will be great."

I wasn't so sure. I wasn't sure if I would ever see any of my new friends again.

After school, I walked back with Francis, my big brother Michael, and some boys from our village. I couldn't hide my unhappiness. Michael came up behind me and gave me a little push.

"Hey, little brother, hurry up! What's eating you?"

"Are we going back to the Sudan?" I asked.

"*I* am," my brother replied smugly.

"What do you mean?" I said.

"All the boys from primary three have been invited to go to a boarding school at Loa. There's a big Catholic church there, and they're taking in students. The school starts at primary four, so only those of us who are graduating get to go. That's what the headmaster told us after the younger kids left."

"What about me?" I demanded. I was beginning to feel a little bit fearful. My best friend, my favorite teacher, and now even my brother were deserting me.

"Haven't you heard? The school at Nyigeri is closing down."

"What?" I couldn't believe it.

"Think about it." My brother spoke more gently this time, feeling my confusion. "The students are gone. The headmaster is gone. The teachers are all leaving. What's left?"

Finally, everything became clear to me. I began to cry. Within days, the school I had been so blessed to attend would be closing its doors forever. I might never get another chance to go to school. I walked the rest of the way home with an ache in my heart. How could I ever see my dreams come true?

That night, as every night, we prayed together as a family. Then my father told us his decision. We would not be leaving Ambuluwa. Our family had invested many years into our home and farm, and we were secure. My father did not want to risk losing everything to return to Sudan prematurely. Yes, there was a cease-fire, but would it hold? My father was very protective of our family, and his decision was to wait and see how things turned out.

"But what will I do?" I asked, unable to conceal my disappointment. "How can I make a difference for our family and our country if I can't go to school?"

"You will need to work as a shepherd again," my father said. "It was good enough for King David; it is good enough for you. Besides, you can't make a difference for anything if you are dead."

I just didn't understand. Father had told us that times were different now, that we needed an education to make a difference. He told us that he didn't want us to end up as uneducated farmers with no influence in modern society. But now he was telling me that I had to give up my dream of an education to take care of sheep and goats. It just didn't make sense.

# Chapter 6

# Changes

THE CHANGES CAME quickly, and they pummeled me like heavy droplets from a sudden squall during the rainy season. I could no longer go to school. My friend Michael Longwa returned to the Sudan. My big brother Michael Odu was packing to go to the secondary boarding school far away in Loa. Neighbors had left their homes eerily vacant in the rush to return from exile.

Then my world was rocked again when I discovered that my older sisters Angela and Jemima, who had been like second mothers to me, were marrying their boyfriends and moving back to Sudan. I couldn't believe that my family was being torn apart, and Mama and Abba were doing nothing to stop it.

In those days, in Ambuluwa there were no telephones, no e-mail, no roads, and no transportation.

Odu, Jemima, and Angela might as well have been leaving for another planet. We would have no contact with them after they left.

And then the worst news of all blindsided us like a raging torrent: Mama became ill—very ill. Severe headaches, weakness, and pain left her bedridden and unable to go about her usual activities.

We had no way of knowing what was wrong with Mama, and there was no medical care available near our home. We only knew that she was gravely ill, and we needed to care for her in whatever way we could. It fell to me to take on the extra chores around the house and to tend to Mama's needs when she asked me. And I didn't mind doing extra work for her, because I knew she would have done anything she could to help any of us kids.

When my older siblings and new brothers-in-law finally left, Ambuluwa truly seemed like a ghost town. Without Mama or the other men of the community to help him, Father was overwhelmed with work. Francis and I weren't old enough to do a man's work, and it took both of us—and our sister Rose besides—just to get Mama's work done.

Soon Father realized that we couldn't continue to live in the wilderness. The work was just too much, and more importantly, we needed to get help for Mama. The only way to do that was to leave our wilderness home.

I was sitting next to Mama, trying to get her to eat some porridge when Father came in and gathered what was left of our family around. "Anna," he said softly, "try to eat something."

Mama just nodded and then turned her head from the spoon that I offered her. I looked up at Father and shook my head. "She only ate a couple of bites, Abba."

Father sat down by the bed and stroked Mama's hair. "I've made a decision," he said. "We're leaving Ambuluwa."

Mama didn't say anything but nodded her assent. As usual, she already had known what her husband was going to say. Rose, Francis, and I didn't argue. Ambuluwa was not the place we had come to love anymore. It was feeling less like home and more like the jungle each passing day, and now the forest would reclaim it.

"Where will we go, Abba?" Little Rose, now eight, asked. She had never known any other home.

"We will go back to Nyigeri, near the main road. From there, we can bring your mother to the UN hospital. Maybe they can help her there."

Although the school in Nyigeri was now closed, people still lived there, and its proximity to the main road into the Sudan made travel and communication possible. Since it was near the border, it was a safe spot to live. If trouble arose in Uganda, it would be easy to slip back across the border and head to Nimule. I knew my father had considered all of these factors carefully.

## Leaving the Wilderness

I was glad to be going. It would be great to be near other people again, but mostly I was relieved

that Mama would be getting help soon. I was beginning to fear for her life.

As soon as we had settled into our new home, the
whole family set off to the UN hospital in Nimule,
South Sudan. The doctors wanted Mama to stay in
the hospital, so for the first time in my life, I went
home without her.

I lived in Nyigeri for more than a year, and it was
not a happy time for me. My mother spent six long
months in the hospital, and for much of that time
we didn't know if she would survive. But God was
merciful to our family, and Mama began to improve.
Eventually she was well enough to return to Nyigeri,
though she hadn't yet returned to full health. Still,
we were thankful to have her back home with us.

## Good and Bad News

My sister Jemima lived with her husband Albereto
Kenyi in Loa, and when Mama had been home from
the hospital for a while, the newlyweds came to visit.
It was wonderful to see the joy on Mama's face
when she saw her daughter again.

"Jemima, I have missed you so much!" It was
wonderful to see Mama able to stand and embrace
her younger daughter. "What news do you have
from Loa?" Mama asked. "How is your brother
Odu? Is he doing well in school?"

A shadow passed over Jemima's face, but she
quickly covered it with a smile. "I have the best
news for you, Mama!" she cried. "I'm going to have
a baby!"

"Ajjugo, did you hear? We're going to be grand-parents!" Mama's smile was so bright that I had to laugh with joy. It was so good to see my sister make Mama smile like that.

Father came up and slapped Albereto on the back. "Congratulations, Son! It's about time!" He pulled up some chairs, and the family sat down to-gether to talk. Father turned to Jemima. "So, Jemima, tell us . . . how is your brother doing?"

Jemima and Albereto exchanged glances. From their moment of hesitation, I gathered that the news was not going to be good.

Finally, Albereto spoke up. "Ajjugo, I have to say that Odu is one of the reasons we came to visit to-day. I'm sorry, but we have to spoil your good news with some bad."

I heard Mama catch her breath. "Is he okay? Is he hurt?"

Albereto shook his head. "I know that you were counting on me to keep him in line, because we live near the school in Loa. I haven't lived up to your ex-pectations. Michael has left Loa."

"What?" My father was stunned. "Odu has left Loa? What kind of rebellion is this? He knows that this family has invested everything in his education. Where has he gone?"

"I am hoping this is only youthful foolishness," Jemima said. "Perhaps he will come back to school. He has gotten involved with some bad friends, and they are involved in drinking and chasing girls. He and some other boys just dropped out of school. We couldn't stop him."

It was depressing to watch the happiness on Mama's face turn to tears. We had all placed so much hope in my brother Michael's education. Now we feared that his life was headed in the wrong direction. I wondered if he had felt too much pressure to succeed.

Father spoke next. "I went through some troubled times myself at his age," he said, clearly trying to encourage each of us. "It was Grandfather Vuni who came alongside me and gave me some direction."

He glanced at Mama and smiled. "I took his advice, and then I married his daughter. We will pray that Odu will accept advice and find his way again. I'm sure that he will come back to us when this time passes. Don't blame yourself, Albereto—he will make his own choices."

After that disheartening news about my brother, we all were determined to dwell on the happy report of my sister's first child.

Eventually, Father's prediction was fulfilled. Although he didn't complete his schooling, Odu did return and claim his important place in our family. But at the time, the thought of my brother throwing away the very thing that I so desperately wanted filled me with consternation. I loved my brother dearly, but it hardly seemed fair that he had the chance to go to school while I was doomed to stay in Nyigeri with no future that I could see. How I wished I could have been in Odu's place at the boarding school in Loa.

## Renewed Hopes

The abandoned school in Nyigeri was a constant reminder that my education had stalled terribly. I was already ten years old, and I knew that if I didn't finish primary school I would have no hope for the future. My only lot in life would be farming, and I would be forced to go wherever the political situation demanded—growing enough food to survive and running from the Sudanese government. I respected farming, and I was not afraid to work with my hands, but even Father was quick to agree that simple subsistence farming would soon become obsolete in our rapidly changing world.

As time passed, I began to despair of ever achieving my goals. It was my two sisters, Angela and Jemima, who finally brought some hope back into my life. Jemima and Albereto had settled near Loa. Angela and her new husband Korica were going to live in Bori near Opari, a region where some of Mother's relatives lived.

My uncle Ezekiel and my maternal grandfather were both teachers at the Opari Elementary School, a new school that had opened up since the return of large groups of refugees. Since Loa was near Uganda, Jemima was willing to take me with her and on to Angela's home. Angela was willing to bring me up to Nyakaningwa, a village in the Opari district, where my aunt and uncle could look after me. If I went with them, I would be able to attend school again at last.

I didn't hesitate. I knew what I wanted to do,

and I begged my father to let me go. At first, he was adamantly opposed to the idea. He was afraid to let me leave Uganda by myself since I was only ten, and he believed that my place at that age was with my own parents. But he also knew that my options were terribly limited in Nyigeri. Angela also argued on my behalf, reminding our father that he himself had told us many times how valuable an education could be. In fact, it was because of his words that I was so eager to pursue an education in the first place. Besides, with Odu out of school, our family's hopes would have to rest on me, the younger son.

Reluctant though he was, Father eventually relented. I was soon on my way back to the Sudan. I didn't realize it at the time, but leaving for Opari would mark one of the greatest changes of all in my life. That decision charted the course for my future and shaped the person I was to become in many different ways. It was a choice leading to independence, education, and great personal pain.

The upheavals that I would experience in my life were only beginning. God would use the changes to break my heart and shape my soul. It was to be an increasingly difficult process, but like clay in the hands of the potter, I would be crushed, cast, and molded into something useful for my Creator.

# Chapter 7

# The
# Bible or
# the Axe

I LEFT MY parents' home with gifts of cloth and peanut butter to bring to my relatives. I was proud that they trusted me to be the bearer of greetings and gifts all the way from Uganda. I hadn't seen my uncle for many years, and I had never met his wife or any of my cousins, but that didn't matter. In our large extended family and beyond, we treated one another as if we were the closest of kin. We were a people who supported each other from community to community with openhanded hospitality. For that reason, I didn't feel awkward when I was received graciously into the home of my uncle. It was the most natural thing in the world for us.

Grandpa Vuni and Uncle Ezekiel welcomed me, and they both thought that it was a great idea for me to come to pursue my education.

"Good to see you again, little William." Grandpa smiled. "You too, Angela, and it's great to see you and your new husband back here where you belong."

We sat down to a festive dinner, with more relatives than I had seen in years. I explained the purpose of my visit between mouthfuls. "I want to go to school again, Grandpa. Our school closed down in Nyigeri."

Grandpa nodded. "We heard about that. Heard your father won't be coming back home either. I wish he would." There was no condemnation in his voice; it was merely a statement of fact. "There isn't much left in Nyigeri."

That was certainly true. "He doesn't trust the government. He thinks everyone will only have to run again in a few years."

Grandpa shrugged. "He's probably right. But in the meantime, I'm going to stay home as long as I can. Who knows, maybe things will turn out all right."

We discussed the latest political events for a while, and then the conversation turned back to me.

"It's been awhile since you were in school," my uncle remarked. "You should repeat primary grade one."

I stiffened at the suggestion. I knew that time was working against me. "I'll be fine," I insisted. "Just give me a chance and I'll prove it to you. Please let me start grade two—I'm nearly eleven!"

Uncle looked doubtful, but he decided to give me a chance. "I'll tell you what," he said. "You can start primary two. After a month or so, we will evaluate your performance. If you do well, you can stay. If not, you will be held back."

The plan was reasonable, and I could do nothing but agree. "I promise you I will do my best," I said.

## Back to School

It was with great relief that I began my schooling in grade two at the Opari school in Nyakaningwa, a village that boasted a population of nearly a thousand. Since it was near the borderlands of two neighboring tribes, many residents spoke both Madi and Ocholi. It was practically cosmopolitan. Sturdy brick-frame buildings topped with thatch lined the single main road—a dirt road that wound its way from Torit to Nimule-Juba in southern Sudan. Big flatbed trucks or Land Rovers would occasionally rumble past on the rutted thoroughfare, and usually the vehicles were coated with thick layers of dust since they dislodged great clouds of the stuff as they traveled.

Local traffic was accomplished with bicycles or on foot. There was no electrical lighting, so we relied on kerosene lamps to ward off the dark; and our water was pumped by hand. Still in all, it was a big city to me. The school building consisted of a single structure divided into three rooms, each with a blackboard. It was very similar in design to my old school in Uganda, except that it was less than a mile from where I was staying. I was glad that I wouldn't have to run seven miles through the jungle to get to class.

I lived with my uncle Ezekiel, his wife Marietta,

and their new baby boy Kanga Wilson and two older daughters, Rose and Josephine. Besides her own three children, Aunt Marietta took care of my cousin Moses and me, as well as Letiyo, a niece from her side of the family. It must have been difficult for her to have to take responsibility for three children who were not her own. It was certainly difficult for us to adjust to life in a household run by someone other than our own mothers. I experienced many moments of homesickness, but I did my best to be obedient to my surrogate parents and to do everything that was expected of me.

I soon found out that my uncle and the other teachers at school were having trouble. The newly autonomous southern government based in Juba was responsible for handling the money for education. Unfortunately, the Islamic government from the North had few funds budgeted for southern Sudanese education. The money that they did release through Juba passed through many hands, mostly those of corrupt officials. So, even though southerners administered the Juba-based government, it did little to actually help the governed. As a result, the teachers at our school went for months at a time with no pay and no funds for supplies. It was purely an exercise in self-sacrifice for the teachers, who freely gave up time that they could have spent growing food for their families.

Occasionally, some staff workers from UNICEF would come by to provide us with books, papers, and pencils. The UN relief did help some, but I be-

gan to see the strain building in my uncle's home.
Feeding all of us was a burden.

Finally, the teachers got together and explained
to the parents of the village that they were not being
paid much, if at all. They held a community meeting
to try to solve the problem. Realistically, the school
would have to be closed down if the teachers could
not afford to feed their families. There was a big
crowd at the meeting, with families attending from
miles around. Everyone had a stake in the success of
the Opari Elementary School.

Working together, we came up with an unusual
plan. Every Friday, the students were required to
dedicate two hours to a physical education curriculum. Gym class was everyone's favorite, but that
was about to change. Instead of the usual running
races and soccer games, it was decided that students
would need to clear land and plant crops. There
were three to four hundred students in the school,
and we all worked together with our instructors
clearing, plowing, and planting a large parcel of un-
used land. It was definitely an unorthodox PE class,
but every week we worked hard planting cassava,
grain, sorghum, beans, sesame, millet, sweet potatoes,
tomatoes, and all sorts of green vegetables. It was
tiring work.

By October, we had reaped a huge harvest. There
was enough food for all of the teachers to eat at last.
We had a wonderful celebration, attended by parents and teachers alike. We came to realize that we
didn't need money from Khartoum to educate ourselves. We didn't need the money siphoned off by

corrupt officials in Juba to feed ourselves. We learned that we could work together as parents, teachers, and students to achieve our common goals.

## The Good Reverend

During the week, I worked hard to complete my studies and grow food. But on Sundays, I had the opportunity to attend the first real church I had ever seen. The African Inland Church, like the school building, was a simple structure. Grandpa had worked hard to restore the building, which had stood idle while congregants spent several long years in exile.

The roof was made of thatch and the walls were plastered with muddy clay. Baked bricks added strength to the structure, and glassless windows let in natural light. The church stood on a hill near the Kulo-jobi River, just a stone's throw from the school compound. I loved going to that small, simple structure each Sunday morning. We didn't need an ornate cathedral or elaborate stained glass, because the beauty for our call to worship came from God's world all around us.

The Opari region was lush and beautiful, with soaring mountains and rushing streams. I loved walking to church on Sundays, enjoying the sights and sounds of the countryside and taking a break from my farming work. But the best part about going to church was hearing my grandfather preach. His sermons were different from the classes that he taught in Christian Education at the school. He made the Bible come alive in a way that made me want to apply it to my life.

My grandfather, the Reverend Andrew Vuni, was the most prominent of all the village elders, and people often sought his counsel. The force of his convictions and the power of the Holy Spirit in his life brought admiration and respect from all who knew him—including me. In my mind's eye, I could imagine him dressed in robes and sandals, holding the staff of an Old Testament prophet in one hand and the scrolls of the Torah in the other. Although he was an old man, his dark skin was smooth and his slender frame stood erect. His rough hands bore testimony to years of hard work cultivating rice and bananas, and of raising flocks of sheep and goats. But it was my grandfather's eyes that I recall most vividly. Those dark brown eyes were serious, sober, and penetrating—they somehow conveyed both sternness and compassion at the same time. I was proud to have Grandpa as my teacher and my pastor. Under his tutelage, I decided to dedicate my life to Yeshua in a real and personal way.

## Naming Our Enemy

When I came to faith, I wanted to be baptized right away. But Grandpa's church required a three-year period of study and preparation prior to baptism, so I was enrolled in a class with several other church members. Grandpa Vuni was our teacher.

During one early session, we studied the apostle Paul's message in the book of Ephesians, chapter six. Pages rustled as students young and old turned to the passage. It was a warm, tropical evening and I enjoyed the cool of the cement floor and the gentle breeze that passed through the screened windows. One of the older students stood to read the passage aloud:

*"Finally, be strong in the Lord, and in the strength of His might. Put on the full armor of God, that you may be able to stand firm against the schemes of the devil. For our struggle is not against flesh and blood, but against the rulers, against the powers, against the world forces of this darkness, against the spiritual forces of wickedness in the heavenly places. Therefore, take up the full armor of God, that you may be able to resist in the evil day, and having done everything, to stand firm"* (NASB).

The room fell silent as we struggled to grasp the meaning of the passage. Grandpa looked around the room, studying faces.

"There is an enemy," he said. "There is one who would erase the name of Yeshua from our country, and would gladly shed our blood to gain his ground. Who can name our enemy?"

Several sets of eyes looked up at the pastor. It was clear that everyone in the room knew who was seeking to destroy us. A hand went up.

"The Muslims of Khartoum are our enemies. They would like to drive Christians from this country."

A murmur of agreement filled the room, until my grandfather silenced it with a wave of his hand.

"No, you are wrong." Grandpa spoke sharply, frustrated that his students were so slow to comprehend the meaning of the Scripture they had just read. "Don't you understand? Our enemy is not human. We do not struggle against flesh and blood, but against spiritual powers. The one who opposes us is much greater than any mortal man, and he wants to destroy Muslims and Christians alike. But it is the name of Yeshua that he cannot abide."

Nobody wanted to ask a question; we were all trying hard to understand without looking stupid. Fortunately, Grandpa Vuni continued his explanation.

"Satan is our enemy. He blinds the eyes of the Muslims to the gospel message. They are left in darkness, bound by the chains of sin. He has beaten them already. He deceives human leaders into declaring war on the innocent, spreading genocide and persecution against God's children. But greater is He that is in us than he that is in the world. Praise God! Satan can kill our bodies, but he can never devour our souls in hell."

All this talk of malevolent spiritual forces made me feel a little frightened. I was glad I was going to heaven, but I didn't want to be killed and get there before my time. Nervously, I raised my hand.

"Since God is greater than the devil, why doesn't He just fight him? He would surely win, wouldn't He?"

Grandpa smiled. "He already did. The battle has been won, and in the most unexpected way. "

"How?"

"The cross, of course. The cross has made it possible for us to pass over from death to life. It's as simple as trusting in Yeshua. Sin, death, and hell have no power over us."

"So why does the Bible tell us to stand firm against the schemes of the devil? Didn't you just say that the battle is over?"

"The battle is won, but it is not over—not until Christ returns to claim His kingdom. We must fight, but our warfare is spiritual. You can't fight a spiritual enemy with physical weapons."

"How do you fight a spirit? Is there a special ritual for that?" One of the older students looked perplexed as he tried to figure out how to fight something he couldn't see. That was something only shamans were trained to do.

Grandpa was treading on delicate ground, and he knew it. Witchcraft was a very real influence among my people, and it was not unusual even for Christians to be involved with the superstitions of traditional magic. Many shamanistic rituals were thought to ward off evil spirits, and my grandfather wanted to make a very clear distinction between the Christian view of spiritual evil and the animist way.

"There is no ritual; there is no magic. There is only the sword of the Spirit, which is the Word of God."

"You mean the Bible is our weapon?"

"Exactly!" Grandpa's eyes brightened as he sensed that his students were finally getting it. "The Bible is sharper than any two-edged sword. Reading it and meditating on it brings power from the Holy Spirit. Prayer and constant connection with God will guard your heart and your mind. You will be given strength to face whatever enemy may come."

I didn't fully understand all of this at the time, but now I know how carefully I was being prepared for the real battles that were to come. Grandpa had lived through a lot of trouble, and like my father, I'm sure he suspected we hadn't seen the end of it. He wanted all of us to understand that our earthly enemies were just people who needed God's love. He wanted us to understand that the war and the corruption and the hunger and the pain and the hatred were just symptoms of the disease of sin. God's overarching plan, I would come to understand, is not about our comfort. It is about His redemptive plan.

Our little class continued, and I gradually came to grasp more about the Scriptures. I moved beyond the familiar stories of the patriarchs and the miracles of Christ and into the more complex ideas of theology, church polity, and Christian living. I had so much to learn, and for three years I dedicated myself to knowing all that I could.

## Wade in the Water

As my education through the primary school progressed, I found that I could read and understand with increasing ability. God really confirmed that my decision to pursue an education was the right one. With flowering literacy came flowering spiritual growth for me. I will never forget the day that I received my baptism. It was a pivotal experience in my life, defining the man I was to become.

The decision that was put before me tested everything that my father and my grandfather had so carefully taught me.

It was December of 1977, and the quiet, brown waters of the Kulo-jobi River lapped and eddied along rocky banks that had been exposed by the long dry season. The dry season was the time of baptism in most villages, because that was when the waters were calm. In August, torrential rains would swell the riverbed, and the Kulo-jobi would rage and boil again. It wouldn't do to have congregants swept away by the currents.

I stood on the shore, a skinny boy of thirteen, feeling the packed dirt beneath my bare feet. Tall grasses bent and rustled as a warm breath of dry air soughed across the savannah lands, mingling the scents of sun-dappled vegetation and hot earth. The mountains stood out in sharp relief in the blue sky beyond the wooded riverbanks. It was easy to think about God's great love for me as I drank in the beauty of my surroundings.

I barely noticed the others from my baptismal group as they gathered by the river. After a brief sermon and a hymn, the ceremony began. When my name was finally called, I walked toward the great tree that served as the cathedral for our outdoor gathering. Its branches spread lazily overhead, swaying softly in the breeze. Huge roots twisted into the riverbank at crazy angles, jutting up like solid benches that were perfect for sitting on.

Grandpa looked into my eyes, and I sensed that he was studying my face very carefully. He was searching for something in my expression, but I wasn't sure what that something could be.

"William Ochan Levi," he said. "Your enemy will come."

I quietly nodded. Without a word, Grandpa produced an axe and placed it on a broad root of the great tree. Next to it, he placed the Bible. Then he turned and focused his gaze on me once again.

"When your enemy comes to destroy you, which weapon will you choose?"

*Would it be the Bible or the axe?* I was taken aback by the question. If my enemies were coming toward me, preparing to kill me, I would certainly want to have that broad, sharp axe in my hand. I could almost feel the heft of the smooth wooden handle, worn by years of hewing trees. I knew what it felt like to send the sharp steel ringing into a sturdy trunk. Surely the axe would give me a fighting chance against the swords of the jihad.

*For our struggle is not against flesh and blood.* . . . The words of my Scripture lessons flooded my mind with a new clarity. Suddenly, I understood that I would never be able to fight my enemy with a weapon of steel.

Almost as if by instinct, my hand reached for the Bible. Grandpa smiled, and I thought I detected a fleeting expression of relief.

"You have chosen the right way," he said at last.

As we waded together into the murky water, I knew that I would have to trust God for my life just as I trusted Him for my soul. I emerged from the water a changed man.

# Chapter 8

# Juba

THE UGANDAN DICTATOR Idi Amin fell from power in 1979, shortly after my graduation from Opari Elementary School. I was busy selling grain to pay tuition costs that spring, and the currency of trade often includes news that travels faster than goods. When I heard the rumors, I knew immediately that the fall of Amin would spell certain disaster for the refugees who were still living in Uganda, including my parents. It was time for my family to return to the Sudan, no matter what the risk.

I literally dropped everything to rush to Uganda to help my family make their escape, and I was not a moment too soon. Thousands of Idi Amin's ex-soldiers, as well as civilians of Uganda and Sudanese refugees were flooding across the border into the Sudan. Armed thugs roamed the streets of Ugandan villages, killing indiscriminately. It was a time of bloody chaos, but my parents and I were able to bring my younger siblings and some belongings across the border to safety in Nimule.

Nimule was a hilly, craggy hamlet overlooking the Ugandan border just at the spot where the river Nile makes its crossing into the Sudan. The only road for miles around threaded a path into the little border town, and Nimule was soon desperately overcrowded with refugees. My parents were among the many who stayed briefly before making plans to find a more permanent home in Sudan. My father still lived in fear of the Islamic regime that dominated our native country, but the threat of renewed persecution and civil war in Sudan was not as imminent as the threat from Uganda's descent into lawlessness. Once again, our family would be forced to make a new start in the wilderness.

During this time, I learned of my acceptance into the middle school at Nimule. I was thrilled, of course, but I had to wait for eight months for the school to open. That provided me with the opportunity to help my parents find a new home.

My father settled on a village called Corom, meaning, "Men are equal." It was a fine spot, surrounded by four mountains and adorned with mahogany trees. My brothers Michael Odu and Francis joined me, and we worked hard to plow the fertile soil and build a new house for our parents.

Mother and Father were very pleased to see how much we had grown and how skilled we had become since they had seen us last. As our little farm took shape, my older brother Michael Odu was reunited with his elementary school sweetheart Katharine, and they decided to marry and settle there with our parents in Corom.

Of the many Ugandan refugees who came up to build homes, one was the biological father of my adopted brother Francis. It was a difficult reunion for Francis, who had been abandoned so long ago, but he was able to forgive. They were finally able to lay aside the hurt of the past and find reconciliation during this time of rebuilding.

## Big-City Life

With my family safely settled in the wilderness of Corom, I was able to enter middle school in Nimule with a sense of relief. Like most middle schools, the Nimule school was, of necessity, a boarding school. Most students had to travel long distances to attend such a regional school, and only the most serious students continued education into the secondary levels.

Life was tough in the Sudan then as it is now, and education was a prize obtained only with great effort. So, for those of us at the middle school, it came as a great disappointment that school was declared over for the year in January due to a lack of food. The policy of the Khartoum-based Government of Sudan (GOS) toward the southern schools was to cut off their supplies in order to discourage southern Christians from pursuing a higher education. Uneducated people are always easier to control and manipulate, and they generally don't pose a threat to the regime.

I was terribly discouraged when I returned to Corom. I felt that the Government of Sudan had once again sabotaged my education. It was obvious that I could not return to Nimule. With all my interrupted school years, I would be an adult before I could attend high school. So after some deliberation, it was decided that I ought to head for Juba, which was some 120 miles north of Corom.

The capital of the "autonomous" southern portion of Sudan, Juba was the first real city I had ever seen. It was a diverse and wealthy community of merchants and traders. The schools there were the best to be found in the southern portion of the country. There were cars, markets, buildings, and people from many different cultures and walks of life. Once there, I needed to find a job, a place to live, and a middle school that would accept me into its program.

My parents had helped me find a place to start— I had gifts to bring for my mother's cousin Gerelina and her husband Nicodemous. I could count on a warm welcome from them.

## Finding My Way

I was glad to discover that my mother's cousin had a son my age named James. Gerelina invited me to stay with her son James until I could settle in to my own accommodations. I accepted gratefully. The following day, James showed me around the Juba area.

I craned my neck to take in the vast expanse of large structures rising from the streets of Juba as far as the eye could see. It was quite a contrast from the towns I was used to, where the only public buildings were the church and the school.

"Several of these buildings are schools," James said, "but I go to that one." He pointed to one of the structures nearby. "It's called Buluk Intermediate School. I hope you get admitted there too."

I shuffled along behind my second cousin, taking in the sights. I asked him if he knew of any local jobs, because I couldn't ask the Nicodemous family to support me indefinitely. Although I was only a middle-schooler, I knew that I would need to be self-sufficient for the first time in my life.

James stopped at a large, open-air market. It was crammed with ranks of dusty people haggling and milling about. The air was heavy with the smell of spices and leather and ripe produce.

"This is Konyo-konyo," he said proudly. "I work here."

I was impressed by the sheer size and the conspicuous wealth of the marketplace.

"Which shop is yours?"

James pointed out a small grocery store. "I sell tea to the customers who come here to buy groceries."

"What are my chances of getting a job in a place like that?"

James looked at me and frowned slightly. "Do you speak Arabic?" he asked.

I shook my head.

"Well, that could be a problem, because most of

the merchants are of an Arab background. It would be hard to get a job in the market if you can't speak Juba Arabic. You need to learn the language first."

James spent the morning introducing me to downtown Juba and explaining the ins and outs of city life. Then I set out on my own, in hopes of finding work.

Juba had a large number of expatriates from around the world, and most of them spoke English. I figured I could find a job with one of these people. Though my only real skill was farming, I knew I could work as an errand boy for a businessman if the opportunity arose.

I wandered through the busy streets, passing stall after stall of merchants hawking their wares. The colorful awnings, the strange smells, and the profusion of exotic items for sale were mesmerizing. For a while, I forgot my mission and fancied myself a window-shopper. I was startled out of my fantasizing by a voice calling my name.

"William!" The voice was familiar, but I couldn't immediately place it. I turned around to see a young man waving to me from a nearby stall. Could it be?

It was Michael Longwa, my childhood friend! His face looked almost the same, but he was now a broad-shouldered, muscular young teenager. I hurried to the stall where he was at work as a salesman. "Michael, it's so great to see you again!"

"Likewise!" he said with his broad smile. "What are you doing here?"

"I came to go to school. I just arrived here in town."

"I'm going to school too. Oh, just a minute." Michael turned from me and began assisting a customer. He spoke in rapid-fire Arabic. I was impressed. The customer completed his purchase and was soon on his way.

"Wow, Michael, you speak Arabic really well."

"You have to speak it here if you want to work for the businessmen."

"So I've heard. I can only speak a few phrases. Where can I find a job around here where I can speak English?"

Michael thought for a while. "Well," he replied, "there are a lot of American missionaries working all over Juba. Maybe you could get a job working for them. Your English is excellent, so I'm sure that would be a plus."

During his lunch break, Michael treated me to a meal at the Konyo-konyo market. We had a good time catching up. First grade in Uganda had only been a few years ago, but it felt like several lifetimes.

Michael told me where I could find the missionary quarter, where there was a compound housing the Summer Institute of Linguistics (SIL). I decided I would try to find a job there.

"I think that is the right decision, but be careful," Michael said forebodingly. "Remember, this is Juba."

I approached the SIL compound with a mixture of hope and unease. I noticed a Land Cruiser just leaving the compound and hailed its missionary occupants to a stop. I explained my situation to the man and woman in the vehicle and asked if they could offer me a job. The woman in the passenger seat leaned out to get a better look at me.

"What kind of skills do you have?" she asked.

"I come from a farm," I replied. "I am good at gardening and tending sheep."

The couple shook their heads. "Sorry, we can't help you right now," the woman said. "We don't have a job for you."

As the Land Cruiser drove away, I felt my future leaving with it. For the next two months, I pounded the pavement in Juba, every day asking for work and every day being turned away. It was a lonely time that tried my faith nearly to the breaking point.

## First Things First

The people of Juba lived a life that I had not been aware of before. There was material wealth in an abundance that made me wonder if God had been holding out on me. It didn't make sense that the people who did not believe in Jesus were so rich and successful, while I was barely surviving. I grew angry with God, and bitter toward the people who refused to hire me. I began to question the teachings of my father and grandfather. It seemed to me that God was not being true to His word. He was not taking care of me.

Despite my bitterness, I turned to the Bible for comfort. It was all I had, and it was all I knew. As I read, I came across Matthew 6:33—"*Seek ye first the kingdom of God, and his righteousness; and all these things shall be added unto you."* Suddenly I knew I was wrong to worry about what to eat, where to sleep, and whether I would go to school. I was trusting in myself instead of believing in God.

After a time of prayer, I went to listen to a street preacher whom I had heard regularly in downtown Juba. His name was Benjamin Terah, and on this particular day he preached on the power of the cross—how it does not change depending on time or circumstance. He encouraged us to bring our burdens to Jesus, and offered to pray for any who were in need. I went forward, and Pastor Ben prayed for me. He told me not to lose heart and invited me to attend the Juba Christian Center where he was ministering.

Two days after my encounter with Pastor Ben, I received word from my mother's cousin Gerelina that my father had arrived in Juba to see how I was adjusting to city life. Unfortunately, he had fallen ill after his long trip from Corom and had to be sent to the hospital for a couple of days. I found him recovering at the Juba Regional Hospital.

"Father, I'm so happy you're here," I said. I told him everything that had happened since my arrival in Juba. He listened carefully and prayed over me. He encouraged me to trust in God's provision, as he himself had learned to do through many years of exile and uncertainty.

He was discharged from the hospital on a Sunday morning, just in time for us to attend church together at the nearby All Saints Cathedral. I didn't normally go there, but it was close to the hospital.

Of course, God had a reason for bringing us there on that day.

After the service, I noticed a foreign couple looking at me as if they had seen me before. They came up to me and introduced themselves as Chuck and Patsy Ohrenschall, from the U.S.A. It was the couple from the SIL.

"Aren't you the boy who came by the compound for a job?" Patsy asked.

"Yes, that was me."

"Are you still looking for work?"

"Yes, I haven't found anything yet."

Chuck extended his hand and I shook it. "It turns out that we need a gardener to manage the property for the SIL compound," he explained. "We're going to be out of the country for a while. Do you think you could handle the maintenance around the place?"

Of course I could! It was the perfect job for me. I was so glad that my father was there to see the almost immediate answer to our prayers.

## Learning to Trust

School had already begun, but now that I had an income, I was ready to register for classes immediately at Buluk Intermediate. I found myself in the same class as my old friend Michael Longwa. But God wasn't finished answering all of my prayers yet.

Pastor Ben heard that I was working at the SIL as a gardener and had been accepted at the school. He offered my friend Severino and me a two-bedroom apartment at the Juba Christian Center. To earn our keep, we simply needed to clean the church and maintain the landscaping of the grounds. All of my prayers were answered even more generously than I could have imagined.

God was not slow to provide for me, I realized; He just wanted me to learn to depend on Him. It was a lesson I would cling to from that day forward.

The next few months were productive ones. Michael and I often studied together, and my friend Severino and I worked as a team at the SIL and the Juba Christian Center. Both school and work were going well for all of us.

Sometimes we would join our new friend and mentor Pastor Ben as he conducted open-air revival meetings in the streets of Juba. Michael dreamed of becoming a minister himself, and I think he learned a lot from all the preaching that we heard in those days. In retrospect, I can see how Pastor Ben was making the most of the time that he had to teach us boys and to reach out to the citizens of Juba. He knew what was coming, and he was preparing us in the only way that he knew how.

It started at the end of 1981. The time had come for Michael and me to prepare for the Senior Secondary School entrance examinations. But what should have been a time of academic testing for young students became a time of political maneuvering and discrimination.

The Islamic regime based in Khartoum set out to undermine the educational system of the south portion of Sudan. Their goal was to impose Islamic rules in all the schools, starting with the Arabic language. The Addis-Ababa Agreement of 1972 had specified that southerners would be allowed to conduct their education in English. Khartoum blatantly broke this agreement with a unilateral decree that all students must be tested in the Arabic language— starting immediately. This was to be a prelude to the introduction of compulsory Koranic education.

I was outraged. Even though I had received near-perfect scores on the tests that I had taken, my inability to speak Arabic left me shut out of the new educational system in Sudan.

I was despondent. I understood then that I was being discriminated against, and there was absolutely nothing that I could do about it. I couldn't understand why God would provide a way for me to live in Juba and then take away my very reason for living there. Something was terribly wrong.

Even so, the lesson I had so recently learned about trusting God had not been forgotten. I went to my employers at the SIL and to Pastor Ben to ask for prayer and whatever assistance they could give me.

After the adults had prayed for me, Pastor Ben spoke frankly to me.

"William, you might as well know that going to the Juba Day School will not be the answer to our prayers," he said.

"What do you mean?" I asked him.

"Khartoum is tightening its grip on the public schools. Before long, they will have you boys memorizing the Koran. Your friend Michael speaks Arabic really well, but I predict he won't be welcome in the public schools for long either. It's coming."

"What's coming?"

"The persecution. The changes. I hear the rumors." Pastor Ben, I learned, used to be a military man, so he kept up on politics. "Khartoum is ready to make a move."

I didn't like the sound of that, so I tried to focus on the present. "So, what should I do now?"

He motioned for all the grown-ups to gather around. "We will pray that William will be able to attend a Christian high school."

A Christian high school? Didn't Pastor Ben know that there weren't any nearby Christian high schools? But he ignored the absurdity of his request and led all of us in fervent prayer that I would be admitted to this nonexistent Christian high school.

To my surprise, I soon learned that a Christian high school *did* exist—and in Khartoum, of all places. The elite of the ruling Muslim class had been sending their children to the Comboni Catholic School in Khartoum for over fifty years. The Verona Fathers were a group of Italian men with excellent skills in science and mathematics. Their school was a preparatory institution for medical and engineering students, and it was the best in the country. Although the Islamic regime rejected the teachings of Christ, upon which the school was founded, they used it to educate their own children. As it turned out, the Verona Fathers had a plan to open a brand-new Comboni school in Juba to benefit the Christian children who had no other hope of education.

## Making the Cut

Testing to enter the new Comboni school took place immediately. The school did not accept the Sudan Intermediate School Certificate that I had so recently failed to obtain. Instead, three hundred students took entrance exams, and Severino and I were among only eighty students to make the cut. By God's grace, I was accepted into an elite high school in Juba without taking Arabic. But God did not just protect my future by providing me with a Christian high school; He put me in the best school in the nation and provided me with tuition.

Work was hard at the Comboni school, but I thoroughly enjoyed it. It was great to have my friend and roommate Severino to study with. The next year, I was happy to see Michael Longwa at Comboni. He had quit the Juba Day School and decided that the Christian school was superior in every way. Another friend from our old village, Gosh Isaacs, arrived in Juba to pursue his education as well. My circle of friends was growing even as my education was flourishing.

My cousin, Rev. John Moi, also ended up nearby, pastoring the African Inland Church. When we didn't attend the Juba Christian Center on Sundays, we enjoyed visiting John's church. It was a great time for me, but there was trouble on the horizon, and the clouds of a great storm were gathering fast.

## Divide and Conquer

During my high school years, the government of Jaafar Mohammed Nimieri was slowly dismantling the Addis-Ababa Agreement of 1972. The autonomy of the South was being dissolved step-by-step. Nimieri divided the South into three separate states in order to rend the tenuous unity between the tribes and stir up old tribal rivalries.

The next step in Nimieri's plan was to move the ministry of education, natural resources, mining, and wildlife to central government control. To reinforce this power bid, he imposed military rule in the South and made a daring move to reshuffle the veteran army of southern Sudan who had fought in the Anya-Nya movement. The regime was poised to conscript all southern boys born in the year 1964 and after to bolster the Islamic army and suppress any opposition to the new regime. Not unexpectedly, there was an uproar in the southern army and in the southern churches as freedoms were slowly stripped away.

There was a military mutiny at Bor, in Jongolei, where the former Anya-Nya army refused to surrender their guns and be re-billeted in the North. They fled into Ethiopia. The rebellion became "official" when the regime attacked their position in the Boma hills and killed eighteen soldiers.

Dr. John Garang, a professor of military academics at Khartoum University, was commissioned by President Nimieri to go to Bor and convince the rebels to lay down their arms and accept their new commission in the northern Islamic army. Since Dr. Garang was himself a southerner from Bor, it was believed that he would have the ability to influence the rebels. Instead, Garang took the opportunity to leave the Islamic regime forever. He joined the ranks of the rebels at Bor and founded the Sudan People's Liberation Army (SPLA), of which he was the commander in chief.

Many southerners from Equatoria were not happy with the formation of the SPLA, because Dr. Garang was a Dinka. Some Dinkas were filled with pride and believed that their tribe was destined for greatness. So squabbling between ethnic groups divided churches and provinces as Nimieri plotted to impose Shari'a law throughout the South.

People who were focused on petty racial differences failed to see the monstrous danger that would crush them all. Shari'a was the real danger.

Churches bickering about local power didn't realize that they would soon have to apply for permission from the Islamic magistrates to congregate in their own buildings. They didn't understand that the Koran would be taught in the public schools and that the Bible would be banned. They had no clue that the churches would be shut down, and the missionary organizations forced to leave the country. Even the Comboni secondary school would be compelled to close if it failed to change its curriculum in accordance with Shari'a law.

Tribes complaining about territorial issues failed to realize that their own young men would be conscripted into the Islamic army. Their enemies would be their own brothers and sisters. To be a good citizen, they would have to take the jihad oath. They didn't understand that land owned by non-Muslims would be confiscated, that Christians would not be allowed to own property unless they paid impossibly high taxes. They didn't realize that all of the natural resources in the South—including land, wildlife, water, and minerals—would be controlled by Islamic law; and the tribes would have no rights over their own ancestral inheritance. Instead, they were riled up about which tribe ought to have the most power.

Jaafar Mohammed Nimieri had planned well, and the pieces were all falling into place. It was time to move.

# Chapter 9

# Shari'a

SHARI'A CAME SUDDENLY, though not unexpectedly. One day we had some illusion of freedom, and the next day we had none. It was almost funny how the new military leadership put a positive spin on the whole thing. They accused the Christian leaders from the free government of being "soft on crime." The Shari'a, they explained, would rid the people of the scourges of alcohol, prostitution, immorality, and all sorts of petty crimes. Christians, they insisted, were hypocrites who failed to enforce the moral code that they claimed to believe in.

The fundamental principle of Shari'a is that freedom disturbs the moral order and fosters crimes against Islam. Therefore, freedom must be ended, along with the permissive Christian philosophy of government. And both were summarily eliminated.

It didn't take long to see the results of Shari'a. There was a sudden rise in the number of amputees, as petty thievery was met with machete justice. A man's hand for a loaf of bread seemed a price too high to pay. But who would dare to say so? The pain of the new law was felt by Muslims and Christians alike. Most of the Muslims were moderates who didn't particularly welcome the religious police into their lives. But they were cowed by the pressure to conform to the Shari'a, because the edicts came from their own mosques. At least the Christians had some reason to expect that some of the laws would not apply to them.

Through the early days of the Shari'a, Pastor Ben kept up his evangelistic efforts. He had developed a program of street preaching that he took to downtown Juba's business district. People from the congregation would accompany him to a street corner, singing songs in Arabic and attracting groups of onlookers. After the singing, Pastor Ben would deliver a gospel message and an invitation to attend the local church. It was a popular ministry, and I enjoyed going along and singing songs for the people who stopped to listen. But it soon became apparent that the military rulers were going to apply the law across the board, and we found that we were bound by the rules of the religious police just as our Muslim friends and neighbors were. We realized that we would be forced to protest the Shari'a if we hoped to retain some measure of our religious freedom. But protest was a dangerous thing.

Pastor Ben was an ex-Anya-Nya-military-man-turned-preacher. As such, he was under constant surveillance. His outspoken criticism of Shari'a and his defiant street preaching made him and the entire Juba Christian Center congregation prime targets of the Islamic government. We were all considered enemies of the state. Pastor Ben and his family were in grave danger, and he knew it.

## "It Has Started"

"Hello, is anyone here?" I was just stopping by to visit the pastor after school one day, but the church office seemed eerily quiet.

A shuffling noise and a *click* came from the small storage room behind the desk, and then a nervous-looking Pastor Ben peeped out from behind the door.

"Oh, it's only you," he said, obviously relieved. He ducked back into the closet-sized room. "You can come out now."

Several men of the church emerged from their hiding spot in the storage room.

"We thought you might be someone else," one whispered.

I must have looked mystified, so Pastor Ben gestured for me to sit down with the rest of the group. "You're old enough to hear this, William," he said. "This is going to affect you and all the students your age. We were just listening to . . . the radio."

He didn't have to explain further. I knew that the men weren't listening to the latest music. Listening to the radio meant listening to the forbidden broadcast of the Sudan People's Liberation Army. General

Nimieri and his jihad forces considered the SPLA treasonous. Just listening to the broadcast was a criminal act.

Pastor Ben leaned back in his chair, folding and unfolding his hands as he shook his head.

"It has started."

*What has started?* I wondered to myself, but I didn't dare ask.

"Where should we stand on this issue?" one of the church elders mused. "We need to pray for wisdom."

Pastor Ben frowned. "I hate this, but I know it has become necessary. When there is war, we can't remain neutral. We have to stand up for what is right."

*War!* So that was what the men were so nervous about.

"Perhaps the war won't touch Juba," another elder remarked. "We could just try to wait this thing out."

"The last war was seventeen years long!" Pastor Ben said. "There's no way we are going to come out of this thing unscathed—or have you forgotten living in Uganda?"

In bits and pieces, I learned the story. Since 1972, when General Nimieri had signed the peace agreement at Addis Ababa, oil had been discovered in the southern district of Bentu. This is what drove Nimieri to use the time of peace to strategize the division of the southern territories and the unjust imposition of Islamic law and martial rule. He had also signed the Egyptian-Sudan integration law that allowed the Egyptian government to build the Jongolei Canal into the southern territory. The canal would drain 90 percent of the Nile water from the swampland of South Sudan's Sudd region into Egypt, with catastrophic results for the people and the ecosystem of that area. Of course, the southern leadership had not been consulted in the matter. The so-called autonomy of the South was nothing but a cruel joke.

General Nimieri was exploiting ethnic hatred and religious extremism to make a grab for the resources of the South while oppressing or eliminating her people. It was bound to spark a resurgence of the civil war, and it finally had.

The first shots of renewed war had just been fired. Dr. John Garang's SPLA troops had attacked exploration and construction companies that were involved in digging the Jongolei Canal. The attacks sent the message that the companies' activities were illegal and their assets would be targeted for destruction unless the construction was stopped.

Finally, there could be no doubt why Nimieri had been building oil refineries in the North. He was making his move to completely conquer the Africans of the southern Sudan. The men of the church had been listening as the SPLA broadcast an invitation to join the resistance.

"Look, Sudan is for all the people, not just for the radical Muslim elite," said Pastor Ben. He had obviously been thinking about this for a long time. "Here in Juba, we have people from different tribes and different religions. We were all happy to live together until the Shari'a came."

Suddenly, the debate shifted into high gear.

"We must not get entangled in this war."

"But Nimieri wants to stir up hate, and that's wrong."

"We have no place in this conflict."

"When he calls for a jihad, many of the Muslims who support us now will feel it is their duty to side with him—even those who hate him and his Shari'a. I say we fight with the SPLA."

"No, that makes us just as bad as Nimieri."

"Not if we are defending our right to freedom—and maybe even our right to stay alive if we choose to keep our faith."

My head was swimming as I listened to my elders discuss the breakout of the new civil war. Pastor Ben was clearly in favor of helping the resistance. But wasn't he a pastor?

Everything my grandfather had taught me about spiritual warfare told me that physical war was wrong. I had chosen to fight my battles with the sword of the Spirit, the Word of God. But now it seemed like things were more complicated than that. I knew that I would eventually be called upon to choose a weapon, just as I had been called upon to choose one at the time of my baptism. Would I choose the Bible when the time came? I wasn't so sure anymore.

I left the church that evening in a state of agitation. Pastor Ben hadn't really answered my questions; he had only managed to raise more pressing ones. There really weren't any black-and-white answers to count on anyway. I didn't get much sleep that night.

I continued to pray, however. And I sensed the Lord leading me to stay true to that choice I had made on the day of my baptism.

## The Ghost House

For the next several months, I worked together with some other students to arrange peaceful protests. Our goal simply was to state our request that religious autonomy and self-governance ought to be restored in compliance with the 1972 treaty. It was an opinion that enjoyed broad support across religious lines.

Even as we worked out our political agendas, we redoubled our efforts to complete high school in a hurry. We knew that if the Verona Fathers had to leave Sudan, we would be out of luck. We were determined to sit for our final exams while we still could. It was exhausting work, but times were desperate.

Every day saw the ranks of jihad soldiers swell, often by compulsory conscription. Every day also saw the mysterious disappearance of people we knew. We didn't dare ask where they were going or had gone, because it was dangerous for us to be aware of anyone who would join the resistance.

One afternoon in 1984, Michael, Gosh, and I organized what was to be our last peaceful protest, although we didn't know it at the time. The war had been going on for nearly a year, and the situation in Juba was becoming increasingly uncomfortable for us. As usual, we gathered together to pray. We asked God to grant us the freedom to worship Him and the freedom to speak the gospel message. God heard that prayer, and He showed me the freedom that I possessed already—just not in the way I had expected.

A large group of students armed with signs and slogans streamed out into the streets of Juba on that day. The mood was peaceful and perhaps a bit naïve in its hopefulness. As hundreds of young people filled the downtown area, onlookers glanced and then averted their eyes as if to hide any treasonous thoughts that may have arisen in their hearts. Only the sun dared to look boldly down on us, and we were warmed by its apparent approval.

We hadn't been out long when the chants of protest died down to a scattered few, and finally silence. The Government of Sudan military forces were headed our way.

As soon as we saw the armed men in their dusty fatigues, we knew we were in trouble. I didn't turn around, but I could hear the rapid footfalls of kids running away as the slow crunch of boots approached. One of the ranking officers stepped forward, his face hard and without compassion.

"Who is in charge here?" he barked.

His words sent another flurry of students running in all directions. Apparently, he wasn't interested in protesters who ran away, because the soldiers stood their ground.

"I am," I said.

Only then did I dare to look around me. I found that I was all alone, except for my friends Gosh and Michael, who stood by me. The commander gestured to a group of soldiers, and I felt a pair of hands grab my arms from behind. I was jerked back with a rough tug.

"You are all under arrest."

I made brief eye contact with Gosh and then Michael as we were taken away. I was relieved to see defiance in their eyes instead of defeat. There was not yet time for fear, though that would come soon enough.

We rode separately back to the ghost house, a place where prisoners were kept for crimes of conscience. It was a simple cinder-block building, nondescript in every way. I tried to read the expressions of my captors, hoping to glean some insight into my fate. I was not rewarded. Their faces only revealed boredom, sly amusement, or thinly disguised disdain.

My enemy had come for me, and I didn't have an axe to wield. I did, however, have a Bible in my pocket. If they took that away, I had another copy in my heart. It was then that I began to have a glimmer of understanding of my role in this conflict. I didn't have to choose my weapon—God had chosen it for me.

The torture began right away. I was led into a dark room that smelled of dampness and cigarette smoke. The blow to my face knocked me to my hands and knees.

"You!" I felt a fist grab at my shirt, pulling me up to a kneeling position. "What do you know about the SPLA?"

I knew what the SPLA was and what their goals were, but that was about all. "I don't know anything about the SPLA," I replied.

"Liar!" The word struck me just as my face received another crushing blow. "Who are the SPLA operatives in Juba?"

I tasted blood as I opened my mouth to reply. "I'm not involved with the SPLA. I am a peaceful student, demonstrating in favor of the peace agreement." It was the truth, and I had nothing else to say.

The commanding officer gave a grunt of disgust as he waved to his men. "Take care of him," he said. Then he turned to me and lowered his voice menacingly. "Whatever you know, we'll find out." With that, he left the small cell.

For the soldiers, the fun was just beginning. I surmised their job was to break my will, a task that they would apparently relish. They were practically gleeful as they measured and cut strips of cable. It was time for a beating.

They stripped me and humiliated me as the blows fell like rain on my exposed skin. I steeled myself against the searing pain in my body, but it was more difficult to steel my soul against the insults and intimidation. Silently, I recited Scripture to try to keep my own feelings of hatred at bay. My mind felt numb, and I struggled to grasp some shred of the gospel to carry me through.

"How can you stand to be a Jewish dog?" One soldier kicked me as if to emphasize my inferiority. "Do you enjoy being a *kafir* pig?" The soldiers laughed and brought down the cable again and again.

Suddenly, the abuse stopped. One of the soldiers

leaned forward, exhaling the smoky contents of his lungs into my face. "You can make the beating stop," he said. "It is very easy. Only speak *Shahada*. Then you will be one of us. You will join jihad."

They wanted me to confess Islam. Of course, that was something I could never do. If I did, not only would I betray my own faith and conscience, but I would also be obliged to kill my own people and burn down their villages. I would just have to accept the torture.

"Jesus said, 'I am the way, the truth, and the life: no man cometh unto the Father, but by me. . . . He that believeth in me, though he were dead, yet shall he live.'" I tried to reply to each of their demands with Scripture. I knew that in the face of brutality, I was being called upon to be a witness for my faith.

*Dear Lord,* I prayed, *don't leave me. Tell me what to say.*

## My Fiery Furnace

After the soldiers tired of their sport, they left me alone in the darkness. I stretched my body out on the floor, feeling the gritty coolness of dirty cement against my wounds. I was too exhausted to think straight.

I was awakened with a sharp kick in my flank. It was still dark in the little room, and I was terribly disoriented. I couldn't tell if it was day or night in the midst of the gloom. I did know, however, that it was time for my daily torture.

This time, they raised the stakes. The soldiers

twisted long strips of wire between my fingers as I watched with dull detachment. I didn't have the energy to feel horrified or outraged as they swung the loose ends of the cable around a beam in the ceiling. With a jarring snap, one of the soldiers pulled the cable taut. My arms shot upward, pulling my body up by my fingers. Intense nausea swept over me as fingers dislocated and a bone snapped from the unnatural weight it was suddenly forced to bear.

As I dangled from cable-strangled fingers, the guards again began to whip me. Once again the soldiers insisted that the pain would stop as soon as I would recite Shahada. Again, I refused.

I recited Scripture over and over again. Psalm 23, John 3:16, the Beatitudes. When presence of mind allowed, I managed to explain snatches of the gospel message. *Love your enemies . . . pray for those who persecute you.* . . . I had to fight to speak those words. But still the punishment came.

The story of Shadrach, Meshach, and Abednego came to my mind many times throughout my ordeal. I imagined the three young men standing in the fiery furnace because of their stand for God. They didn't know if they would survive the flames. They believed that God was able to deliver them, but they understood that He might not choose to do so. Even so, they made it known to the king that they would never deny their God. They simply could not bow down to Nebuchadnezzar's golden image.

But my will was weakening. If I recited the words of the Shahada, I would become a Muslim. That act would relieve my body from the torture.

I tried to picture myself in the fiery furnace. The burning pain of buffalo-hide whips licked against my skin like flames. Then I remembered that there was a fourth person in the furnace that day, and the fourth man was in appearance like the Son of God. I came to understand that my only weapon was a spiritual one and that I was using it to fight for my very soul. How could I fear men who could destroy my body rather than God, who could destroy my eternal soul? I would not recite Shahada.

I couldn't say how long I remained in the ghost house, not exactly anyway. But eventually the abuses stopped. They were satisfied that I really didn't know anything useful. It was obvious that I was not a danger to their regime.

As I waited for my release, I recalled the prayer that I had prayed with my three friends just before our capture and imprisonment. We had prayed earnestly that God would grant us the freedom to worship Him. In that moment, I understood that God had answered my prayer. I was free to worship now, and I always had been. Now I knew that nothing could force me to do otherwise—not even death.

# Chapter 10

# Close Call in Kapoeta

THE WHITE HAZE of the noontime sun was painfully bright to eyes that had become accustomed to the constant gloom of the prison. I stood for a moment, disoriented by the sights and sounds of the city. How long had I been locked up? It couldn't have been more than a couple of weeks, but it seemed like time had somehow been suspended.

I felt like I was sleepwalking, unsure if I was really headed back to my Juba apartment. The dust was real enough, and the spicy smells from the marketplace were just as I had remembered. It wasn't until my hand stretched out to open the door to my own room that I realized I was definitely awake.

A stabbing pain shot through my hand and up my wrist as my broken and swollen fingers fumbled with the latch. I winced and struggled to push open the door with my forearms instead. It would be some time before I could be back at work attending to the landscaping or holding a pencil at the high school.

"William, thank God you're okay!" I recognized Michael's voice immediately. "I heard the news that they let you go. Thank God!"

My old friend looked bruised and disheveled, but his broad shoulders were unbent and his smile was as genuine as ever. "They let me out this morning too."

"Can you believe this, Michael?"

"They want to make an example of us," he said. "They want everybody to be afraid to speak up. It doesn't matter if you are just a student. Nobody can disagree with the Shari'a law."

"I'm sure they knew we weren't SPLA members. Otherwise, they wouldn't have let us go. But to be honest, I'm still scared. Do you think they can force us to join the Islamic army?"

"They can kill us if we refuse, that's for sure."

"I would rather die than kill one of my own brothers," I said.

"Me too. There is no way I would agree to fight my own people. I would die first."

"That may be what they have in mind."

"So what do we do now, join the SPLA?" Michael said.

The idea was tempting, but I shook my head. Many Christians had already gone off to fight in the guerrilla-style warfare that was being waged against the military regime, but I felt a different call. "We

could, but I don't think that is what God wants for
me. I don't condemn those who fight, but I really believe that I must love my enemy. The sword of the
Spirit has got to be my weapon."

"Well, we can't stay here anymore, that's for
sure," Michael said. "The school is going to be shut
down, and they'll just round us up and try to force
us to fight."

I thought for a while. The heat of the day was
making my swollen hands throb. I had to go lie
down in my own bed and rest. But an idea had come
to my mind.

"Michael, why don't you and Gosh come over
tonight? I think I have a plan."

## Hatching a Plot

I was sore and exhausted, and it felt good to be
back in my apartment after the torture and humilia-
tion of the prison house. Gingerly, I rinsed my
wounds with cold water and straightened out my
bent fingers the best that I could. I changed out of
my dusty and torn clothing and sank down onto my
cot. I must have slept through the entire day, because the next thing I remember was a knock on the
door.

My head pounded and my vision blurred as I
stood up to answer. I could barely walk, because my
whole body was stiff as a board. It was Michael and
Gosh, and they had brought some food.

"Thought you could use some supper," Gosh
offered.

"Thanks." My stomach was sour from being empty for so long. The pain in my hands lent an edge of nausea to the discomfort.

We gave thanks for God's mercy in letting us go free, and then we ate in silence. We all felt discouraged because the prospects for our future didn't look too promising at that moment. But at least we were alive and free—for now.

"So, William, what is your plan?" Michael said.

"Yeah, if you have any brilliant ideas, we're with you," Gosh added.

"Well, we already know that we cannot complete our education here," I began.

Gosh and Michael nodded their agreement.

"What use are we without education? Our people will have no one to lead them."

"No one but the military," Michael quipped.

"That's right. The military leaders are educated, but they will get old or maybe get killed. What will we do when none of us from the South has an education?"

Gosh shook his head. "Nothing, I guess."

"We will be farmers or soldiers—nothing more. There is no way we can help our people that way."

"We will just be forced to live under the Shari'a law," Michael remarked grimly. "That hasn't worked out well so far."

I continued. "If we want to preserve our way of life, our faith, and our people, we have only one choice. We have to get out of the country and get an education."

There was silence for a moment as we all considered the implications of my plan. It was definitely risky, but if it was successful, the benefits would be great.

"Where do you think we should go?" Gosh wondered.

"Kenya," I announced. "I've already considered a route."

Michael Longwa smiled. "I have a brother in Kenya! Mark left for Kenya a year ago to get his pastoral degree, and we can join him up there. Maybe we can all get a fresh start there, and Mark will help us adjust to life in Nairobi. I think it's a great idea."

Gosh looked more hesitant. "You know, William, the SPLA has camps across the Kenyan border. How would it look, three guys like us crossing into Kenya?"

"I know. It would look like we were going to join the SPLA." That was the one concern I hadn't mentioned.

"If they catch us . . ."

"It is a risk we have to take." I was determined to make our escape work. "We have to have a story to tell in case we get captured," I said. "Michael, we can tell them that we are headed to visit your brother but that we'll be returning to Sudan soon. If we rehearse our story ahead of time, our stories will all match. But that is plan B. Plan A is that we don't get caught."

Gosh was looking more and more doubtful. "I prefer plan A," he said.

We all laughed in spite of ourselves and got

down to the business of planning our route and modes of transportation.

## Dangerous Journey

We wasted no time in taking care of loose ends. We said our good-byes to good friends we had come to know. Our friend Pastor Ben, with his family, had already left town to join the SPLA as a military chaplain. Many students were headed back to their hometowns. As it turned out, there wasn't much left to leave behind. Our school was closing down.

Soon I found myself back in Corom, explaining to my parents that I would be leaving the country. The tensions of Shari'a were already being felt even in our remote village.

My parents knew that open warfare could not be far behind. To them, this knowledge was just another fact of life. They were very realistic, and they had learned to deal with oppression and war in a practical, no-nonsense way. It was just a matter of survival for us. Our lives had been lived on the move as refugees for so long that my flight to Kenya to finish school didn't seem like anything new to my family. The fact that my trip would be risky and dangerous was acknowledged but not dwelt upon. Everyone agreed that my idea was a good one, and my family supported my decision fully.

Our trip to Kapoeta—our point of departure—was relatively uneventful. We purchased seats in a crowded, open-topped Austin lorry (motortruck) carrying sheep, grain, and farmers to Kapoeta. We brought next to nothing in the way of personal belongings. But we had some cash (280 Sudanese pounds) and our Bibles with us. We put Michael Longwa in charge of the money, since he had been working as a cashier in Juba. I was assigned the responsibility of decision making and leadership. And Gosh was given the responsibility of monitoring travel logistics.

When we arrived in the small border town, we had suffered nothing worse than a bumpy ride. We knew that the difficult part of the journey was yet to come. Even though we were a mere stone's throw from Kenya, getting across the border would be tricky.

"This place is crawling with GOS [Government of Sudan] military," Michael whispered.

It was true. Dusty olive green lorries prowled the streets, and soldiers with AK-47s slung across their shoulders seemed to be everywhere.

We went over our story again, just in case the soldiers stopped us.

We needed to hire another lorry to take us into Kenya. This, of course, was easier said than done. We kept together, chatting casually, but still feeling all too aware of the ubiquitous GOS soldiers.

Anyone might be a spy, and although there was a constant stream of travelers through Kapoeta, we knew that we could easily arouse suspicion. We purchased lunch at a crowded stall and kept our ears open for possible contacts. With a few discreet inquiries, we soon found what we were looking for.

Michael was the outgoing one. He was a smooth

talker who always seemed to gain a good reception with people. We let him do the bargaining while we hung back, trying to blend into the crowd.

He found someone who was willing to sell us berths on a lorry bound for Kenya. It was leaving town that afternoon. We were all relieved that things were going so smoothly. At this rate, we figured to be in Kenya by nightfall.

That afternoon, we headed downtown to catch our ride. *So far, so good.*

We didn't notice the gradual movement of men in olive drab until we were surrounded. With the cold steel of GOS assault rifles pressed against our backs, we were led away.

The lorry would be leaving without us.

## Captured!

I can hardly recall our trip to the military barracks. I was numb with dread, because I knew we had been branded as SPLA operatives. And our backup plan was likely useless. I realized they weren't going to believe a word we said, no matter how similar our stories sounded. If they thought we were planning to join the SPLA, as they obviously did, we were lost. Being an SPLA member, of course, was a capital offense. But even if we weren't SPLA members, they still wouldn't feel any remorse about our deaths.

Our lives were utterly unimportant to them, whether we were telling the truth or not. A few more dead Christians could only be a good thing in their way of thinking, especially if the dead Christians were young males who had the potential to lead or fight. It was then that I understood that Michael, Gosh, and I were dead men.

It's funny what you think about when you know you are marked for death. Perversely, I was filled with regret that I would not be able to go to school. When you are seventeen, you have your whole life ahead of you. But for me, the desire to finish school was the first thing that came to my mind. Michael and Gosh were silent—I wondered what they were thinking. From their somber expressions, I knew that they were fully aware of the seriousness of our situation.

As expected, the three of us were separated for interrogation. If we had any hope at all, it was for all of us to stick to the story that we had planned. If any of us admitted that we planned to leave Sudan permanently, it would be a death sentence. Leaving the country was tantamount to siding with the SPLA. Even so, there was little hope that we would be believed, no matter what we said.

I was led into a small room without windows. It was empty except for a couple of folding chairs and a light fixture. I was directed to one of the chairs with a shove. The chair tipped back with a lurch as I sat down hard. My thoughts finally cleared enough for me to breathe out a prayer. *Lord, help me.* It was all I could manage under the circumstances, but God understands the inaudible cries of our souls and knows what we would ask even before we can form the thoughts in our consciousness.

My thoughts were jolted into focus with a sharp

blow to my face. An army officer was bending over me, threatening me with his gun.

"Why do you join the SPLA?"

It was not a question I could really answer. I wasn't joining the SPLA, but they would not believe that. I remained silent.

"Answer me! Who are you planning to meet when you join the SPLA?" The officer questioning me narrowed his eyes, his face betraying no sign of compassion.

"I am not joining the SPLA," I finally said. "I am a high school student, but my school was closed down. My friends and I were planning to visit family in Kenya. That's all."

The officer didn't like my answer. I felt another blow land on my cheek. "I want names of your SPLA contacts. Tell me who supports the SPLA, and maybe you will live."

I could answer him honestly, but it was no use. "I don't have SPLA contacts. I don't know anything."

Of course, I knew many people who supported the SPLA ideologically—that would include most southerners. But he probably already knew that.

"Kafir! You infidel traitor." The officer's face reflected his unadulterated disdain. "You and your friends will go to Juba tonight. There you will be tried as traitors. The penalty is death."

My interrogator turned on his heel and left me alone in the little room, guarded by an armed soldier. Although I had already imagined the worst, it was unsettling to have my fears confirmed. I was going to be tried for treason as an SPLA operative. The trial would be a mere formality, and I would be executed, along with my two best friends.

While I was alone in my cell, I had a little time to gather my thoughts and pray. I prayed for myself, my friends, my family. I prayed for my people and my country. I prayed that I wouldn't be tortured again.

As I despaired of any escape from execution, my prayers seemed to bounce off of the ceiling and fall flat on the dirty cement floor. But I knew God heard me, and some hope remained within me.

That evening, my friends and I were herded onto a lorry as prisoners. Several soldiers accompanied us aboard the truck, bound for Juba. There we would be recognized as the student leaders who had protested Shari'a, which would certainly not help our case in our trial for treason. Our only hope for life would be conversion to Islam and a pledge of service to the jihad, but for us death would be the preferred option.

We allowed our eyes to meet briefly, communicating volumes before we looked down again. We didn't dare speak to one another in the presence of our captors. I could see Michael's lips moving slightly, and I knew that he was praying silently. I closed my eyes and joined in, agreeing in wordless prayer. The dusk was passing to darkness as the lorry jolted forward on the road to Juba.

## An Unexpected Turn

Gradually, the faces of my friends faded to outlines and then shadows as the light waned. I could hear the shuffling of feet as soldiers and prisoners shifted positions in the hard seats, and I could see the occasional flare of red when one of the soldiers took a drag off his cigarette. Although I was exhausted, there was no way to rest. My mind continued to form prayers, sometimes coherent and sometimes not. Occasionally, rough spots on the road would jolt painfully up my spine as the lorry's wheels dipped and bounced. The constant grating noise from the old diesel engine made my head throb and my ears ring.

We had been traveling perhaps three or four hours when the lorry's engine noises suddenly increased in pitch from a grate to a whine. I could feel a new vibration shake the old truck so that my teeth rattled. Over the din, I could hear the soldiers complaining to one another in Arabic. Then, without warning, the engine sputtered and died. The lorry ground to a halt along the rough path that served for a road.

It was a moonless night, black as pitch. There was cursing and more shuffling of feet as the soldiers pulled on the parking brake and lifted the hood. I heard the driver call to the cigarette-smoking soldier, something about a light. Inexplicably, the soldiers who had been guarding us hopped off of the lorry and went around to the front of the vehicle to help inspect the engine. For that uncertain moment, we were left unguarded.

The three of us needed no further prompting to know that this was our cue. Without a word, we jumped from the back of the lorry and ran blindly into the darkness. In the few seconds it took for the soldiers to register the sound of our feet hitting the ground, we had already made some distance. There was shouting and confusion among the soldiers, and a few seconds later we heard the sound of assault rifles. Although the shots were fired in our general direction, there was no way the soldiers could see and aim accurately in the blackness. We were all fast runners, used to sprinting through the wilderness. Raw fear lent us speed and sharpened our senses as we ran. I could hear my friends nearby, crashing through the underbrush, and I used the sound to guide me.

In the back of my mind it registered that the shouts of the soldiers were increasingly distant. I knew they were giving chase, but they were running blindly too. We had a head start, and we were running for our lives—without guns and gear to weigh us down. I can't say how long the soldiers chased us, but I know we kept running long after they had turned back. They were probably more concerned about the inconvenience of spending the night in the middle of nowhere with a broken lorry. It would be a long walk for them in the morning if they couldn't repair it.

## Answered Prayers

We ran until we thought our lungs would explode from exertion, and then we gradually slowed to a walk before daring to stop.

"Where are we?" I managed, scarcely able to spare the breath to speak. We had come to a clearing, and

there were only a few landmarks, revealing themselves as dark upon dark in the starlight. I guessed
that we had been running for a few miles.

"I know," Michael panted. "We are only a few
more miles from the town of Torit."

"You can lead us?" Gosh asked.

"Yes, my mother's house isn't far."

We traveled quickly and carefully, sticking close
behind Michael. Although we had run for several
miles, we didn't feel tired. The buzz of adrenaline
kept us hyperalert as we headed back, escaping certain death. Time seemed suspended as we traveled,
but it couldn't have been too long before we reached
Michael's mother's house. It was the middle of the
night, so we knocked on the door as gently as we
could.

Michael's older brother Wilson opened the door.
We saw that the house was lit; and it was full of
people crying and praying, with their faces to the
floor. Michael's relatives looked up, and from their
expressions it seemed as if they had just seen a ghost
—or more accurately, three of them.

"Michael!" His mother ran to embrace him,
tears streaming down her face. She held him close
and sobbed.

"Praise God!" someone exclaimed. "It's them!
They're alive!"

Spontaneous shouts of praise rose up from the
impromptu prayer meeting. Their prayers had just
been answered.

"We heard word from Kapoeta," one of the people
explained. "It was just rumors. They said you were

captured. We were told that you had probably already been executed. We were all here praying for you until we could hear more news."

"God spared us," I said. "We were about to be executed."

The people gathered around us as we recounted the amazing events of the day. It could not have been coincidental that a houseful of people had been interceding for us at the very moment that the lorry's engine died. God had brought the truck to a stop at the darkest hour of the night, within running distance of that very house. The added miracle of being left unguarded, if ever so briefly, confirmed that God had been protecting us. The evening vigil of tears and intercession was immediately transformed into a time of thanksgiving and relief.

The flood of emotions that washed over us diffused the tension that had kept us going for so long. When the tears subsided, we were drained and exhausted. Our sleep that night was deep.

When we awoke the next morning, Michael's mother made us breakfast. Although she was grateful that her son was alive, it was obvious that she was angry. After we had eaten, she spoke her mind.

"William," she said sternly, "I hold you responsible for this reckless idea. My son was nearly killed."

I couldn't blame Mrs. Longwa for feeling upset. Jihad forces had murdered her husband, a pastor, two years after Michael was born. Michael was her baby boy, and she couldn't bear the thought that the same fate might befall him.

"I'm sorry," was all I could say.

In truth, I was sorry we had been caught, but I still believed that escape to Kenya was our only viable option. There were many who planned to just maintain the peace and get by, hoping to live through the troubles unmolested. Mrs. Longwa was hoping to do just that. From past experience, I thought that her particular mind-set was dangerously naïve. It was like sitting in the middle of a lion's den, hoping the beasts weren't too hungry. Eventually one would get eaten. Similarly, everyone in the southern Sudan would discover that the time to take defensive action was past, and they would be running for their lives again. Personally, I planned to be out of the country before I was forced to run, kill, or be killed.

Gosh and I thanked Mrs. Longwa and said goodbye to Michael. Michael's mother forbade him from trying to escape again. He was planning to lie low for a while and see what happened. He respected his mother's wishes and trusted that God would provide a way for him to attend seminary someday in the future. We wished them the best and headed back to Corom.

After a couple of days with my family, Gosh and I also parted company. He went to Moli where his family was staying at the time. Word of our ordeal had traveled quickly, so my parents were not surprised to see me. My father came out to welcome me, draping his arm around my shoulders.

"I'm sorry you didn't make it to Kenya," he said. "The Lord has other plans for you this time."

"I'm not sure what to do," I admitted.

"You can start by thanking God for protecting

you," he said with a grin. "I'm not afraid for you, because nothing will happen to you unless God permits it. I believe that with all of my heart. That's how I keep going in times like this."

"Believe me," I said, "I'm learning to understand that more each day. But how do I know what God has planned for me?"

Father's face turned serious. "Sometimes you just have to pray and then make the best decision that you can. I think God honors that."

I paused for a moment. "I've been thinking—I feel like if I try to escape again, it will have to be alone. I can't take the responsibility for the lives of my friends."

"That sounds reasonable," Father agreed. "Besides, it may be easier to escape if you go alone. You would be less likely to be noticed."

"But what should I do now? I need your advice."

He nodded. "You have had a very close call. I can see why you feel uncertain." He thought for a moment. "I will ask your grandfather and your uncle to come and talk this through with us. God uses the wise counsel of men when decisions are tough. I think they can help you to make the right decision."

"Thanks, Abba."

I felt relieved. I was grateful that my father had not reacted like Michael's mother had. I knew I could count on him and Grandpa to give me their best advice. As we walked into my parents' house, I relished the welcome I received. For one day, I would enjoy the comfort of my family again. Their familiar faces were so precious to me, especially after having come so close to losing my earthly life. There would be time enough for difficult decisions in the morning.

# Chapter 11

# The Eye of the Enemy

WHEN MORNING CAME, my family gathered as promised to help me decide what to do next. We reviewed my options systematically, and the first decision that I felt absolutely certain about was that I needed to complete my education if I ever hoped to really help my family and my nation.

With that decided, it was clear that I would have to leave the Sudan, because all of the educational opportunities in my native country had been closed to me. It was also evident that I could only travel to a country adjoining my own without due process from the authorities—and I was quite sure they wouldn't grant me leave to travel abroad. That left me with an increasingly limited set of options.

"What about Kenya?" I looked around the room, my eyes resting on the concerned faces of my uncle, my father, and my grandfather in turn.

Their expressions were grave as they considered that option. We had already determined that I could not head for exile in Uganda. Ever since the fall of Idi Amin Dada, Uganda had become a bloody killing field. With rampant and random violence, no one could be safe in Uganda anymore. Kenya, however, was relatively stable politically. But would it be possible for me to escape through another border town like Kapoeta?

"Out of the question," my father replied.

"I have to agree with Ajjugo," Uncle Ezekiel added. "The entire Kenyan border is crawling with GOS military. Everyone knows that the SPLA uses Kenya and Ethiopia for their bases, and Kapoeta is a border town adjacent to both countries. That gives the GOS surveillance reason for very high alert in that whole area, if they think you are crossing to join up with the opposition."

"Yeah, I found out the hard way," I said. "I'll be blessed if all they do is kill me."

Truth be told, I already knew that Kenya was not a viable plan. After my capture at Kapoeta, it was obvious that the military had stepped up security there to the extent that crossing into Kenya was a fool's errand. The border routes were carefully guarded because they expected boys like me to head that way. They expected it.

"What *don't* they expect?" I mused.

"What do you mean?"

"The GOS. What *don't* they expect me to do?" I was thinking of a plan, and it was just crazy enough that it made my heart race. I smiled grimly. "They won't expect me to walk through the very eye of my enemy."

My father sought my gaze and found it. He knew I was thinking of something we hadn't discussed before. "What is your plan?"

"It isn't quite a plan yet, but I do have an idea," I answered. "Where are the military units stationed?"

Grandpa Vuni leaned forward. "They're all over the place!"

Father smiled. "They're all over *South* Sudan. . . ." He was beginning to see where I was going with this.

"How many people head to Khartoum to join the SPLA?"

"Khartoum!" Grandpa sputtered. "That is the headquarters of the GOS! No one in his right mind would go there to escape from the jihad forces."

"Exactly," I said. "They would never expect me to make my escape via Khartoum. They would never suppose that I was an SPLA agent if I traveled openly and boldly to the Muslim capital."

Uncle Ezekiel nodded slowly, letting his mind process this new option. "Where would you go from there? You can't stay there, you know."

"You could travel north to Egypt," Grandpa suggested.

"Of course!" I liked that idea. "There are many Sudanese students on scholarship in Cairo, and many businessmen travel there as well."

"No one would accuse you of joining the SPLA by crossing the Egyptian border. Perhaps you could find work there and wait for the situation to improve."

I nodded, wondering briefly what I could do in

Egypt. My Arabic wasn't too great, but maybe I could work as a laborer until—until what? In my heart, I knew that I ultimately wanted to reach the United States. But I knew that religious freedom and economic opportunity were a world away.

I remembered the song I had learned in primary school back in the Ugandan wilderness. It was a song about learning English and getting an education so that I would be able to help my people. Even then, I knew it would take a miracle for me to escape the destiny of so many of my classmates. For us, life was war and survival. Still, I dared to hope for a nobler purpose in my life. The first step was getting out of the country.

## A New Hope

"I will travel north and escape to Egypt," I said. "From there, I will wait for the Lord's direction."

Murmurs of assent arose around me. It was decided.

"Mama, I need to tell you something."

As my mother passed by the open doorway, I motioned for her to come closer. From the look on her face, I knew that she already had a pretty good idea what it was that I was about to say. It was hard to tell my mother that I would be leaving again. Even though she understood the peril that we all faced, it was very difficult for her to accept my decision to leave, especially after my run-in with the military in Kapoeta. She listened quietly as I explained my plan.

"From Egypt," I concluded, "I hope I will be able

to get a visa to travel to the United States. The universities there are the very best in the world, and people have freedom to think as they please. When I get a good education, I will be able to help the family."

Mama looked uncertain. She had no knowledge of geography at all. She couldn't picture in her mind where I might be headed. All she knew was that the U.S. was somewhere very far away.

"You will come back as soon as you can, right, William?"

"Yes, Mama," I replied quietly. I avoided the directness of her gaze. "As soon as I can."

That night, my father took me aside. We stepped outside into the warmth of the evening air. The lingering scent of firewood mixed with the earthy musk of the tall grasses and tilled fields surrounding the village. I breathed it in, memorizing the sensation of living with my family in the Sudan. My father rested his strong arm loosely across my shoulder. We were silent for a while, each of us wrestling with emotions both deep and unsettling.

"William," Father spoke at last, "you know we might never see you again."

Of course I knew.

"Your mother and I want you to know that we love you, and our prayers will follow you even when we don't know where your path has taken you."

I nodded.

"You will always be with your family, because your family is the body of Christ. Wherever you go, find your family first."

My abba was releasing me, and I knew that this

was difficult for him, as it was for me. I listened carefully to his words, because I knew in my heart that I might never receive counsel from my father again. That thought entered my soul like a great weight, crushing my spirit with its gravity.

"Tell Mama not to worry about me," I said with a bit more bravado than I actually felt. "I will be careful, and God will be watching over me. She will be proud of me someday."

Father chuckled. "You know she is proud of you already. Don't you worry about Mama. She may fret about you children sometimes, but she is a lot tougher than you think."

Word travels fast in the small, close-knit communities of the South Sudan. Over the next couple of days, well-wishers from every family had stopped me to express their interest in the success of my journey. I spent my remaining time in Corom visiting with relatives.

The following Sunday, my last at home with my friends and family, Grandpa's little church was packed. At the end of the service, I was asked to stand up and share a brief testimony. As I stood at the front of the little church, I looked out over a small sea of familiar faces.

*These are my people,* I thought. I was overwhelmed with a feeling of love for them, and I gathered renewed strength in the knowledge that it was for them that God was calling me out of Africa. I addressed the crowd from my heart.

"Brothers and sisters," I began, "God is calling me to leave my precious homeland. I will be facing uncertainty and danger. But those of you who remain behind will also be facing tremendous difficulty."

There were heads nodding across the room, as many understood what lay ahead.

"When I received my baptism, Grandpa Vuni asked me to make a choice. He asked me to choose the weapon I would use to face my enemy—the Bible or the axe. I chose the Bible, which is sharper than any two-edged sword."

A few amens rose from the congregation.

"I believe that God has called me to use the Scriptures to fight this war that we're in. I feel that God has a plan for me, and I believe He will use me somehow to bless you, my people. I don't know how that will happen, but for me it will not happen through violence. For that reason, I must leave you. I beg you all to pray for me, and I will pray for you all as well."

When I was finished, the congregation surrounded me to offer up prayers. And then Grandpa pronounced the Aaronic blessing over me.

*"The Lord bless you and keep you. . . ."* The whole congregation joined in the familiar words, and I soaked in every syllable. *Please be gracious to me and give me peace,* I prayed.


## The Last Good-bye

All too soon it was time to leave Corom. My family sold a field full of crops for cash, enough to purchase a one-way airplane ticket to Khartoum with some left over. I was grateful for my parents' sacrifice, and I told them so. Then I said good-bye to Abba and Mama. It would be the last time I ever saw them on this earth.

As the little propeller plane flew at a low altitude over the South of Sudan, I kept my face pressed to the coolness of the double-paned window. I watched as the green of the savannah and the gently rolling foothills gave way to flat, featureless desert. In the distance, the Nile River snaked ever northward, bordered on each side by verdant patches of irrigated farmland. The glare of hazy sunlight reflecting off the sand and refracting through suspended dust made my eyes ache and my head throb. Still, I kept my forehead pressed to the glass. The pressure on my skin counterbalanced the heaviness in my heart. It was a relief to me that no one seated near me was eager to talk.

Eventually, the hum of the engines and the vibration of the narrow but comfortable seat lulled me to sleep. When I awoke, I was in another world. I was in Khartoum.

I had been right about Khartoum. I was unnoticed and unmolested. From there, I caught a train to Wadi Halfa, a small border town in the northern desert between the Sudan and Egypt. Travelers of every description frequented the town, and I was able to purchase a ticket on a steamer bound up the Nile toward Egypt with no difficulty. It was a crowded, unregulated ship, typical of those used in developing nations, and I had the cheapest berth available. We were herded aboard like so many cattle, but I didn't care. I was bound for Egypt.

The engines chugged, and the big ship creaked and groaned to life. With a great heave, we headed north through the confluence of the Nile. It was a slow boat; there was no doubt about that. I had nothing to do but watch Sudan go by. At first it was fascinating to watch the banks of the Nile pass by, patches of green on either side giving way to shimmering white desert. But after a long while, the scenery all started to look the same.

I was bored and uncomfortable, so I took to reading my Bible and singing softly to myself to pass the time. I spent two days aboard the steamer, with nowhere to lie down to rest. It was blisteringly hot beneath the desert sun, and the crush of merchants and traders aboard the ship only made things worse. Most of the time, I kept to the upper deck, which at least provided fresh air and a place to sit.

It was a relief to disembark in Aswan, Egypt. I changed the little money that remained into Egyptian pounds and purchased a train ticket to Cairo. My escape from Sudan had been blessedly uneventful, and for the moment, I was safe. I was just another face in the crowd, jostling for a seat on the crowded train. The air was hot, dusty, and close; and the limited seating made my legs ache, but all of that didn't matter. I was headed for a new life, wherever God would lead me.

# Chapter 12

# Hotel
# Baghdad

I BREATHED A SIGH of relief when my train finally rumbled to a stop in Cairo. It was a great metropolis, bustling with strangers speaking a language I could barely understand, but to me it was a first step on my journey to freedom. *Thank You, Father, for keeping me safe so far.*

I found myself in the Attaba section of Cairo, with only a couple of Egyptian pounds in my pocket. I was exhausted and hungry, with nowhere to go. I wandered through mazes of narrow, winding streets, taking in the sights and sounds of the city as I fought off the heaviness of fatigue that weighed down each step. I knew I would have to find a place to stay and someone to help me find work—but where? I didn't know anyone in the whole of Egypt.

*Lord,* I prayed, *I'm counting on You. Show me where to go. I need Your help.*

I wasn't quite sure if the quickness of my pulse was due to the excitement of adventure or just plain anxiety, but I took a deep breath and tried to focus. The ground seemed to spin and sway as crowds of people passed by in every direction with swirls of colorful clothing and hints of exotic scents. When I looked up, I saw a dusty sign hanging from a dilapidated old building. "HOTEL BAGHDAD," it proclaimed in English. I decided to go inside.

As my eyes adjusted to the darkness, I could appreciate that at one time this five-story structure had been a fine hotel. For now, I was just grateful to discover that this dingy old place was somewhere I could afford to stay, at least for a day or two.

My room was a tiny cubicle furnished only with a cot. The cot had only a plain cotton mattress with no sheets or bedding. That fact was most likely a blessing in disguise, because the place was absolutely filthy. Bedding would surely have been heavily infested with a variety of vermin. There was no running water, and the toilet facilities made me shudder. Though I had never been acquainted with luxurious living, I had always been scrupulous about cleanliness and hygiene.

*Beggars can't be choosers,* I thought to myself as I finally lay down to rest. Indeed, I was fortunate to have a place to lay my head, and I drifted into sleep quickly.

The following day dawned dusty and hot. Dust motes hung lazily in the haze of morning light, like an unspoken challenge to face the difficulties that lay ahead.

I made my way down to the lobby, feeling a bit dazed and unsure of myself. Suddenly, I felt a jovial handclap on my shoulder, rousing me from my reverie.

"Welcome to Hotel Baghdad," a stranger boomed, extending his hand in greeting. "You look like you aren't from around here."

I looked up and attempted a smile. "Yeah. My name is William. I came up from the Sudan."

"So, what brings you to Cairo?"

I was a little wary of confiding in this man. He looked like he might be Arab or perhaps Persian, but he seemed friendly enough. I decided to risk it. "I'm on my way to America. I'm looking for freedom."

The man chuckled. "That's a big step for a young kid like yourself. How old are you, sixteen?"

"I'm eighteen," I replied.

Bit by bit, my story came out. I explained the situation in the Sudan and told him that I was fleeing because of my Christian faith.

"I feel that God's weapons are spiritual. I can't join the jihad and fight my own people, and I don't wish to take up arms with the SPLA either," I explained. "God has given me a different path to follow, with God's Word as my weapon. That's how I ended up here in Cairo."

The man was quiet for a moment. "You truly are a stranger in a strange land, William," he replied at last. "So am I. I am also a Christian believer. I came here from Iraq. Things aren't so great for Christians there either."

"At least we know that this world is not our true home," I replied.

"Well said!" The Iraqi man paused and glanced up at a sign hanging above the registration desk. "Baghdad," he said softly, "reminds me of my home in Iraq." A shadow passed over the man's features for a moment, and then his face brightened again. "This isn't exactly the Ritz, is it, my brother?"

I had to laugh, and I assured him that I had no intention of staying at the Ritz anyway. We chatted for a while, and I marveled that God had provided me with a fellow Christian who could speak English just exactly when and where I needed him—right in the middle of a ramshackle flophouse in Cairo!

"Listen, William," he said after a time, "I know someone who may be able to help you. There is an Anglican church by the name of All Saints Cathedral not too far from here. Maybe they could help you find a place to stay and some work to do."

I thanked him, and the fresh hope he had given me lightened my steps. I soon found myself at the entrance to All Saints Cathedral.

## Uneasy Encounters

Once again, God provided for me in a miraculous way. The pastor of All Saints Cathedral was aware of a group of South Sudanese students who were attending Cairo University on scholarship.

These students came from Christian families and were likely to be willing to take me in.

When I arrived at the apartment where the students lived, a young man named Martin greeted me. He introduced me to his roommates. I was happy to discover that the students all spoke Madi. These young men had all grown up not far from my own village. God was truly good to me. My new roommates were curious about my reasons for leaving Sudan, and they gathered around to ask questions.

"William, why are you in Cairo?" one queried. "You don't attend university here."

Another was equally skeptical. "Are you sure you know what you are doing?" he asked.

"Why leave home with nowhere to go? You don't know what might happen to you," another enjoined. "You are lucky we are here to help you out."

"Yes, and of course you will have to help out with the expenses."

I assured them I would help with expenses, and I began to explain my reasons for leaving my home. I soon found that my new roommates were unaware of the trouble that was brewing in the Sudan. They had special scholarships from the South Sudan government, and they had been isolated in their own world at the university. Even worse, I discovered that they had abandoned their Christian faith and were only superficially interested in following God, if at all. Their lifestyle was similar to what might be found on "fraternity row" in the United States. The pursuit of alcohol and women was more important in their lives than the pursuit of holiness. I would soon find out just how difficult it could be to keep myself pure in such an environment, as a young teenager so far from home.

In the evening, it was not unusual to find my new friends drinking beer.

"Have one, William!"

"Uh, no, thanks, I'd rather not," I said.

"*I'd rather not,*" my friends mocked, chuckling amongst themselves. "For Pete's sake, William, one beer won't kill you."

"Actually, it might," replied another, looking a bit more sober than he was. "But I'm just going to have to take my chances."

I was perplexed. "What do you mean? Beer might kill you?"

"Yeah. Don't you know?"

"Know what?"

"The religious police. They poison the beer."

"What?" I couldn't believe what I was hearing. "That can't possibly be true!"

"Oh, yes, it is," they replied. "Some of the super-religious ones hate drunkards so much that they sneak around putting poison in beer. We know of people who have died from drinking it."

"And you still drink it? Aren't you afraid?"

"Well, it isn't every beer. We figure the chances of getting poisoned are pretty low."

"Yeah, we're not afraid to drink. Everything in life has some risk involved. Why give up our fun?"

I didn't know what to think. I had always respected the Muslim stand against drunkenness, but this was shocking. My friends seemed to be willing to risk their lives for a few hours of fun. Were the pleasures of drink really worth such a high price? I have to admit, there were times when I was tempted to find out.

One night while my friends were drinking, there was a knock at the door. It was a prostitute, offering her services to all of us. I was stunned to discover that my friends entertained such women from time to time. These beautiful young women were willing to give themselves away for as little as two Egyptian pounds. It was an offer almost too good to resist. In my pocket I could feel a few Egyptian pounds that I had received from my new job in a downtown supermarket. More than enough to pay what this woman was asking. Enough to make me forget my loneliness, if only for an hour. None of my companions would judge me, as they were emptying their pockets themselves. My family never needed to know. But God would know, I decided. I could not sin against my own body. It was a difficult decision, but I knew what I would have to do. I would have to take a stand.

"Friends, you know that in the book of Proverbs it says that you are not to join yourself to a prostitute."

"You've got to be kidding!" one of the students said.

"No, I'm serious. God does not want us to dishonor our bodies in this way. Our bodies are meant to be His temple."

"Mind your own business, you little prude."

"Yeah, you don't have to be such a religious fanatic. We're not doing anything wrong."

"You think just because you can't have any fun, we shouldn't either."

"But . . . " I had barely opened my mouth to protest when I was interrupted again.

"Maybe William isn't a man at all!" one of my roommates remarked sarcastically.

Now it was getting personal. My friends were laughing and ridiculing me. I didn't know how to respond.

By this time, everyone was enjoying a good laugh at my expense. My face burned with embarrassment and fury. Involuntarily, my fists clenched and unclenched as I resisted the sudden urge to respond in kind and escalate the conflict. To them it was harmless fun, but I was feeling the pain of ridicule. I knew that if I wanted to maintain my witness for Christ, I would just have to let it go. But how could I remain friends with young men who rejected the values of their Christian faith so easily? I needed some time to pray and ask God for help. I remembered that we ought to give thanks in all circumstances, so I thanked God for His wisdom in providing me with roommates from among my own people.

*God*, I prayed, *please bless each and every one of my friends from the Sudan. Please give me a spirit of love instead of bitterness. Show me what to do!*

God gave me a desire to reach out to my roommates, and He gave me the idea to reach out to a prostitute at the same time. He showed me that He loved prostitutes and prodigals, and I knew He wanted me to feel the same way. Before long, I had a plan in my mind of what to do the next time a prostitute showed up at our door. I just needed to get my roommates to agree to try it.

## "Change My Life"

After our argument had blown over, I approached my friends with my idea. "Guys, I have a way we can help the next prostitute who knocks on our door," I began.

"You mean you plan to buy what she's selling?" one of the students jabbed. A snicker passed through the group of men.

"No, I'm serious," I said. "Just hear me out."

"Okay, William," Martin agreed. "We're listening."

I looked around the room at all the skeptical faces. "Listen, do you think the prostitutes want to do what they are doing?" I asked.

"It's just a job," someone replied. "They're working girls."

"Yeah. They are happy for the business. They need the money."

"Do you really believe that your own mothers and sisters would be happy if they had to sell themselves just to survive?"

Nobody had an answer for that one. My roommates suddenly appeared to be very interested in looking at their shoes.

"I say that the next prostitute that comes by, we give her some money but we don't take advantage of her. Then we'll see what happens."

"What? She will laugh at us—she will think we are fools!"

"Maybe so, but give me a chance. If she laughs at us, I will never complain to you about this again." I had to admit, it did sound outrageous. But I knew God could use it.

My roommates were intrigued by my crazy plan. Actually, they probably were only interested in watching me make a fool of myself, but at least they were listening. We agreed to try my little experiment at the next available opportunity.

We didn't have to wait long. That very week another prostitute knocked on our door, soliciting business. I invited her in.

"Would you like something to drink?" I offered her some hot tea as she slipped into our apartment.

She nodded but kept her eyes lowered and her veil wrapped tightly around her head and shoulders. My roommates' eyes were fixed on me, registering an expression somewhere between morbid curiosity and disbelief. Quietly, they took their seats within easy earshot.

"Have a seat." I motioned to an empty chair near our common table.

The woman reminded me of a shadow sinking in the twilight as she obliged. She dared a glance at my face, as if to question the terms of our encounter. Ever so slightly, her eyes moved to calculate the number of men in our group. With any luck, this would be the only door she would have to knock on this night. I smiled at her, in a ridiculous attempt to feel more at ease, and I took a seat across from hers.

I cleared my throat nervously, without risking a glance at my friends. I figured they would be smirking at me.

"I am wondering," I began, "how a fine Muslim woman like you came to visit us tonight in this way. Please tell us about yourself."

The woman stiffened in her chair, and her complexion paled a bit. This was certainly not a part of the bargain.

"What do you want from me?" she demanded. Her nostrils flared slightly, like a spooked horse, and I could tell by the pulse at her neck that her heart was pounding. She had good reason to be terrified. The only thing worse than the abuse and indignity she suffered from her customers was the prospect of being brought to justice in the courts of Islam. I suspected that if she were ever caught, the law would not be too forgiving.

"You are informants!" she declared. "I will not speak to you."

"I give you my word, we will not turn you in. We do not wish any harm to come to you. In fact, we want to help you. I am a Christian. My beliefs allow intimacy only within the sacred bonds of marriage. I know that as a Muslim, you also value chastity."

The woman's shoulders relaxed a bit, and her gaze dropped to hands that were folded primly in her lap. She pinched her lips tightly together. "I have children, you know."

"Go on."

"I love my children more than life. . . . " She looked around the room, seeking empathy—or at least understanding. "I must care for them. What can I do?"

It was not a question meant for answering. Postures shifted uncomfortably as my roommates tried not to think of how they took advantage of women like her. Slowly, the woman's story came out. It was not easy for us to hear, or for her to tell. My friends remained silent as stones.

I turned to her and extended my hand in friendship. "We don't want anything from you. You don't need to sell yourself to us."

I gathered together ten Egyptian pounds and pressed them into her hand. "On behalf of all the men in this room, take this money and go home to feed your children. This is the beginning of good things happening in your life."

The woman initially stared at me with her mouth agape, and then her slight frame was racked by uncontrollable sobs. Tears filled her dark eyes until they slipped slowly from her lashes. She never had reason to expect kindness from anyone, especially men.

"God loves you; that is why we are helping you," I said. "Jesus can bring you forgiveness and healing. But you must want to change your life. With God, all things are possible. Would you like me to pray with you?"

"Oh, yes," she whispered. "I do want to change my life."

After the prayer, she dried her eyes, accepted my prayers and the money gratefully, and left in peace.

My roommates were stunned and convicted by

what they had seen. It was awhile after the woman had left before anyone found the courage to speak. Finally, one of them took the initiative. Grinning sheepishly, he slapped me on the back.

"William," he said, "I hate to admit it—but I guess you were right."

"Yeah. Maybe you aren't such a fanatic after all."

The episode with the prostitute proved to be a real turning point in the lives of several of my room-mates. It was quite disturbing for them to look at that woman as a real person and not an object for sex—to see the consequences of their own sin in the life of a poor, destitute mother. The Holy Spirit con-victed them of their need to live lives of compassion and purity. Some prayed for salvation and some rededicated their lives to Jesus.

I was reminded once again how God has a good plan for everything in my life. The discomfort I had experienced due to the ridicule of my friends was to-tally eclipsed by the joy of seeing Christ at work in their lives.

Still, I sensed I could not remain there much longer. I was acutely aware of the fact that I was de-pending on their hospitality, since I was not attend-ing the university as they were. My job at the supermarket didn't pay much, and I began to realize that there was no way I was going to save enough to purchase the necessary visas and airfare to reach the United States. There was restlessness in my spirit, and I knew that I would need to make a change soon.

# Chapter 13

# Madame Seiko

FOR TWO MORE MONTHS, I threw myself into my job at the supermarket with vigor. My relationship with my roommates had improved, and I was still able to pay my share of the expenses. Even so, I knew in my heart that the time had come for me to move on. The students I was living with had helped me when I had nowhere else to go, but they had not planned to take me in permanently. Finding another apartment in Cairo would be costly. Work at the grocery didn't pay well, and my back ached from standing at the register for twelve hours every day. I felt like I was in a holding pattern, unsure of the next step God would have me to take. I knew that I had served God's purpose as a witness among my new friends from the Sudan, and that knowledge confirmed in my heart that a new purpose was coming soon.

I was at work one day, feeling unsure—and feeling pretty sore—when I took a brief break from register duty. I pressed my hands to my lower back to work out the tension, and let out a little groan.

"Hey, William," I heard someone say. "Are you having a rough day?"

It was Edward Ibrahim, a repairman who often came to the supermarket when the old refrigeration system went on the blink. He was a Coptic believer who was outgoing and helpful, and I enjoyed talking to him whenever he stopped by.

"Good morning, Edward," I said with a bit more cheerfulness than I felt at that moment. "My back is just acting up today. It bothers me when I stand here too long. I guess I'm not cut out for this type of work."

"Why not look for a new job?" Mr. Ibrahim suggested. "You are young and educated. I'm sure you could find something that suits you better."

Mr. Ibrahim paused for a moment, resting his hand on his tool belt. "I know a lady who needs someone who can read and write in English, but she lives outside of Cairo a fair distance."

I wondered if God was about to show me a new direction to take. "Tell me about it," I said.

"Her name is Madame Seiko. She's a Japanese lady, and she runs a farm. You can tell her that I'm willing to vouch for you, and she'll listen to you. You're a good kid. I don't think you will have any trouble there."

I thought for a moment, gathering resolve. "Thanks, Mr. Ibrahim; I think I'll do that."

He gave me the information that I needed and then turned back to his efforts at refrigerator repair.

Later that day, I found myself on a train headed for Madame Seiko's house. She raised dairy cows in the countryside near Cairo. As soon as I saw the farm, I immediately felt at home. All of my life I had cared for animals and worked the land. That little bit of familiarity caused a twinge of homesickness.

Although I had only been away from my homeland for a few months, I had a bitter realization that I might never see my home or my family again. I remembered the look on my mother's face as she gave me her blessing for my journey to freedom, knowing full well that she might never see me again. Even though my emotions were in some turmoil, I approached Madame Seiko with confidence to ask for employment.

I was certain that working on a farm again would be good for me, and I looked forward to using my English skills in a new way.

As it turned out, Madame Seiko was eager to hire me. "So, William, when can you start work?" She was a sharp businesswoman, and I soon discovered that she was always quick to get to the point.

"I can begin right away, but . . ." I hesitated. There was a request I needed to make, and I didn't know if my prospective employer would be too happy about it. "I can only work for you if I can take Sundays off."

Although Madame Seiko was married to a Muslim man, and was therefore considered to be a Muslim herself, she really cared very little for religion of any sort. Friday was the expected day of religious observance in this Muslim community, and I knew it might throw things off schedule if she were to grant my request. Even so, I knew I could not compromise on this issue, because I was sure that I would be devastated without any contact with fellow believers. Madame Seiko was silent for a moment, considering my unorthodox request. Finally, she acquiesced.

"Very well, William," she said. "I see no reason why you should not live as your religion dictates."

"Thank you, Madame," I said. "I promise to do my best for you and the farm."

## Life on the Farm

True to my word, I began working right away and was quick to learn the skills I was required to master. It was comforting in a way to work once again in an agricultural setting. I was thankful that God had provided me with another job. Just as I had found more than I bargained for with my wayward roommates in Cairo, I soon discovered that life in this rural community was going to be a real test of my Christian faith.

The problems started the very first week. As the other farmworkers were entering the compound for another day of hard work, it was immediately evident to them that I was headed elsewhere. Since my boss had approved my Sunday departure, I felt that I had nothing to hide. As I walked two miles to the train station to make the trip to Cairo for worship, I was feeling pretty happy. I was eager to spend the day at church. But by the time I got back from the city, it was already dark, and it was pretty late by the time I finished the long hike from the station back to the compound. Rumors spread quickly in a small town, especially about a foreigner. The other men had noticed that I didn't show up for work at all that Sunday, and it didn't take them too long to find out why.

"*Kafir!*" The word hissed from man to man as I passed by to get to my work the following Monday. Although I was not fluent in Arabic, the word sent chills down my spine. The other men were calling me an "infidel," someone who was worthy of being stoned to death.

"You are a lazy dog, kafir," one of the men yelled from across the barn. He stared at me with contempt in his eyes. "You refuse to work like a man on Sunday, and instead you go to wallow in your filthy idolatry."

I stood frozen in my tracks, my eyes searching quickly for a way to escape. I did not want a confrontation, especially in the darkness of the barn with so many sharp farming tools within easy reach. A couple of men, also interested in avoiding trouble, hurriedly quit the scene as if they suddenly remembered how much work they had waiting for them outside.

Another farmhand spat in my direction. "Who do you think you are?" He stepped forward, and his muscular forearms tightened menacingly. "You take a job that should have belonged to one of us, and then you go to lie around with those Western devils while we do your work."

I shuffled backwards toward the barn door, not daring to turn my back on the men. I hoped that I looked calm, but my alarm must have been obvious to them as they moved slowly toward me. *Lord, help me,* I prayed silently. I knew that I was no match for the two angry men, and I didn't think any of the other workers would step in to defend me.

"William!" The commanding voice of Madame Seiko summoned me from outside the barn. "I have a job for you; come now."

The two farmhands scowled as they turned away. I knew that, as far as they were concerned, our little "discussion" was far from over.

"Thank You, God," I breathed quietly, "for getting me out of that one!"

I hurried out of the barn, grateful for the bright sunshine and open space of the outdoors. I made a mental note to check carefully before going into the barn or other dark outbuildings. I had a feeling I was now a marked man. Madame Seiko stood near a new tractor, smiling proudly.

"My new tractor," she said. "I want you to learn how to use it. It will be your responsibility."

I looked up at the shiny new piece of equipment. It would be fun to learn how to operate and maintain, and I was already looking forward to the task of driving it. I was chosen for this special job, I learned, because I was the only one able to read the English manuals that came with it. I took the instructional materials from Madame Seiko.

"I'll study these manuals right away, ma'am," I said.

I hopped up into the metal driver's seat and found that it was surprisingly comfortable. I paged through the glossy technical guide, noting each gauge and lever as I went along. It was absorbing, interesting material to me, and I soon had a good idea of how the big machine was supposed to work.

Before long, I was ready to take the tractor for a spin. I put the rig in gear, and soon I could feel the rumble of machinery vibrating up through my hands and down my whole body. I threw the gearshift into drive, and I was off.

The rest of that day was spent tilling the fields with the new tractor. I was careful to ride in neat, precise rows, keeping the plow lines vertical to the gentle slope of the terrain. The warm, freshly turned earth smelled comforting to me. The land was a good and constant gift from God. And honest labor would generally bear fruit even in the most troubling times. By nightfall, I was ready to rest.

After supper, I retired to my quarters. They were spare but clean and comfortable. I was able to spend some time reading my Bible and singing quietly to myself. After the frightening encounter with the Muslim farmhands, I understood that life on the compound was not going to be easy for me. I could not neglect to nurture my spirit, because I sensed that forces of darkness were preparing an attack. Forewarned is forearmed, and it was very clear that I would need to arm myself for a spiritual conflict in the days ahead.

## Trying to Cope

*Father, I know that these men are not my enemy. My true enemy is Satan. Please give me the strength to be a witness for You to these men. I know that You love them. Help me to never return evil for evil, so that You will be honored.*

It was hard to feel God's love for men who hated me and hated my faith, but I understood even then that love is not a "feeling"; it is a decision. Love is obedience to God's will toward other people. As I tried to put away all bitter thoughts, I didn't realize that there was far worse yet to come.

The remainder of the week was fairly uneventful. I took every opportunity to prove myself to the other workers. I worked very diligently and tried to help others at every opportunity. I felt like I needed to compensate somehow for my absence on Sunday and prove that I was not lazy.

Some of the workers were grudgingly responsive, and I tried to fit in by speaking to them in Arabic. By listening and speaking, I began to feel more comfortable with the language, although I was still unable to read or write it.

Finally, the end of the week came; it was Friday, the Muslim day of prayer. I realized with sudden dismay that all of my hard work to fit in with the other workers would be tried to the breaking point on this day. When the call to mosque came, I felt my heart sink. *What will the others think of me when I don't show up for prayers?* Of course, I soon found out the answer to that question.

"Blasphemer!"

I looked up from my work to see the men returning from their prayer time. Their faces burned with indignation. "You blaspheme Allah by refusing his call to mosque!"

The man who had threatened me earlier that week confronted me again. His beard trembled as he spat out the words, "There is no God but Allah, and Muhammad is his prophet. Do you believe this? *Do you?*"

I knew that I didn't have the answer he was looking for, so I remained silent. I was sitting up in the tractor, so at least I felt safe from physical assault. I turned the key, and the motor rumbled to life. As I maneuvered the tractor toward the field, I could hear the epithets following me. I tried not to listen. The ethnic and religious insults were hurled at me like sharp knives. I was a pig . . . a dog . . . an infidel . . . a blasphemer. I should go back to Sudan where they would really "take care" of me.

*Why, God? Why are they doing this to me?* I knew in my head that Jesus said, "I will never leave you nor forsake you," but in my heart, I felt very alone. Everything about me set me apart from my peers in the village. My appearance, my language, my culture, and especially my faith kept the others either at arm's length or overtly hostile. I wondered what purpose God could have had in mind when He sent me to be the only Christian for miles around. Does God really work all things together for good to those who are called according to His purpose? To be honest, I was having doubts about that one. I was isolated, I was in danger, and I had nowhere else to go. *What can I do to get out of this situation?* I thought to myself.

I couldn't go back to Sudan—I would be forcibly conscripted into the jihad. I couldn't go to the U.S.—I didn't have the money or the proper paperwork yet. I couldn't even go back to Cairo—I couldn't live with the students again, and I would be unemployed. I missed my family terribly, and I knew that they had no idea where I was.

To make matters worse, the news about Sudan that I heard on the radio in bits and pieces wasn't good. Villages were being attacked and burned to the ground. Factions were fighting. Random shootings and violence were spreading throughout the region. I longed to know what had happened to my family members, but I had no way of finding out.

Night after night, I found myself crying in the darkness of my little room, asking God to help me. It seemed like He just wasn't listening. As days became weeks, and weeks became months, I became increasingly depressed. I held on tightly to God and spent my evenings studying the Bible and praying. Life on the farm was becoming increasingly difficult for me.

## Good Cop, Bad Cop

There was a young man about my age named Nabil who didn't threaten me, but he would often argue with me about the error of my ways. He was a sincere believer in Islam, and we had several discussions about issues of faith. Since I was progressing rapidly in my ability to speak and understand Arabic, I was able to converse with him fairly readily.

"William," he said, grasping my shoulder as if he was planning to shake some sense into me, "why do you refuse to accept that Muhammad is the seal of the prophets? Don't you see that to worship the man Issa is blasphemous? There is no God but Allah, and he will punish you for the worship of a man."

"You are correct about one thing, Nabil," I replied. "It is blasphemous to worship a mere man. But Issa—Yeshua—is not a mere man. He is God incarnate, God with us."

"Your Bible has been corrupted—it has been perverted. Although it does contain God's revelation, the Koran is God's pure word. It is the perfection and completion of the religions of the Jews and the Christians."

"Our Bible is very reliable," I insisted. I was feeling a little agitated. "There were hundreds of ancient prophecies about Issa from the Old Testament that came true many hundreds of years later! The historical accuracy of the Scriptures is being proven every day by archaeologists!"

"Christianity is propaganda of Western missionaries. You are being brainwashed by the Europeans and the Americans. You should accept the true religion of your people—Islam!"

"My people are the Hebrews," I said. "They lived right here in Egypt." I didn't like the implication that the great *I AM* who revealed Himself to Moses not far from this very place was a "foreign"

God. ". . . And Jesus Christ came to save the whole world—not just Westerners or Jews or Africans—everyone! Jesus told us to go into the whole world to preach the gospel. The Western missionaries are following the orders of a Palestinian Jew! Islam is not the 'true religion' of Africa, or anywhere else, for that matter!"

It was becoming apparent that neither one of us was going to convince the other to change his beliefs; but at least we could have a discussion about the issues, and I was grateful for that. I was also grateful that my Arabic skills were improving to the point where I could converse fluently with Nabil. I felt like I was beginning to understand his beliefs more clearly, and I hoped he was beginning to understand mine. Although we did not agree, I felt that he was trying to help me in his own way. He believed that I would really be better off if I became a Muslim.

Although there was no intellectual temptation for me to accept Islam, the social pressure to become a Muslim was almost more than I could bear. While Nabil argued with my intellect, an older man named Saide argued with my heart.

Saide was a relatively wealthy middle-aged family man who also worked on Madame Seiko's farm. He wanted to take me under his wing and get me to listen to reason. He was a calm, friendly man, and he was very pragmatic.

"You know, William," he said to me, "I see that you are a hardworking young man. Madame Seiko has given you a lot of responsibility."

"Thanks," I mumbled, although I wasn't quite sure what he was getting at.

"Why do you insist on living the life of a kafir in our village? It will bring you only pain."

*Well, he's got that much right,* I thought to myself. I had plenty of pain and then some to spare.

"You are very young; you do not live with your people anymore." He leaned forward, his brow crinkled with earnest concern. "You could be happy here. You could have a nice car and a nice home. People would accept you if you would just accept Islam."

The way he said it made it seem so simple, like buying a new pair of shoes so as not to get blisters on my feet.

"I can't reject my faith," I replied. "It is everything to me. It is my life now and in eternity."

Saide laughed. "Allah will take care of you if you follow the Koran," he said. "Why worry about eternity when your life is so miserable today?"

I had to admit that he had a point there. "My life is not too great right now," I agreed.

"I have a beautiful daughter who is just seventeen. If you accept Islam, she could be your wife. You could have children, and you could have a good life. I will give you a car for your wedding. If life proves difficult for us here on the farm, we could all move to Fayum, the town in southwestern Egypt where my family came from before we moved here to work for Madame Seiko. What do you say?"

The beautiful daughter part sounded pretty good, and I was desperate for security and acceptance. Would I ever have a good life? Should I just give up trying to serve Yeshua and live in peace? Life in the little farming village outside Cairo could be happy. I loved working the land and milking the cows. The families were close-knit and peaceful. It wasn't really so different from the life I had known with my own family in the wilderness of Uganda, after all. If I were to become a Muslim, I would be welcomed into the community, and my skills would be valued instead of resented. The timeworn tactic of "good cop, bad cop" was definitely having an effect on me. On one hand, the "bad cop" villagers would use threats to induce me to recant my faith in Christ. On the other hand, the "good cop" villagers were kind to me and offered pleasant rewards as inducements to convert. Saide's offer of marriage and prosperity was very tempting.

At that point, I was so worn down that I was close to giving up and becoming a Muslim. Then I remembered the story of Jacob and Esau. Esau sold his birthright for a mere bowl of stew. The exchange was outrageously one-sided. How foolish Esau was to forfeit his blessing for a fleeting satisfaction. God spoke to me through that Scripture story. Did I really want to trade my salvation for human acceptance? How could I sell my inheritance and forfeit my soul? I felt God's sharp rebuke. As weary as I felt, and as much as I wanted a wife and family, I knew I would not—*could* not—give up my faith.

## Emerging from the Darkness

I said no to Saide's offer. I worked through the rest of the day like an automaton. My heart felt so heavy, and God seemed so far away. I didn't react at all when the farmhands insulted me. I didn't even have the heart to care. It was just another miserable day. I was so out of sorts after work that I didn't even think about carefully choosing my path home. I just walked in a direct path, without looking in every direction as had become my habit. My carelessness was a big mistake. Before I knew what was happening, I was ambushed.

"There's the blasphemer; let's get him!" someone yelled. "Yeah, the dog has become Madame Seiko's little pet! She lets him have the easy life riding on the tractor and taking Sundays off."

I felt the first punches fall sharp and heavy on my chest and back. I tried to breathe, but the wind was knocked out of me. I struggled to twist free from the painful grip that twisted and bruised my flesh.

"You don't deserve to work here, kafir," a voice growled into my ear. "You don't even deserve to live!"

The beating I endured was horrible. But the physical pain was nothing compared to the dark shadow over my soul. Finally, I broke free. My breath came in quick, shallow sobs as I struggled to get back to my room. I fell exhausted into bed and slept a troubled sleep.

The one blessing I felt during this dark time was that Madame Seiko consistently treated me with fairness and respect. She kept her promise and allowed me to travel to Cairo each Sunday. As I rode the train toward Cairo, I felt a cloud of oppression lift from my shoulders. I was like a starving man as I entered the fellowship of the saints. For a few brief hours, I felt alive again. The trip back to the farm, however, was another story.

I was practically sick with dread as I returned to my personal place of torment. Walking the final two miles back to the farm from the train station was like the walk of a condemned man to the gallows. I knew the persecution that awaited me when I returned would continue to escalate. I was beginning to fear for my life.

I will never forget what happened one Sunday night after I got off the train on my way back to the farm. The night was very dark and I was tired. It was not just a physical exhaustion; it was a deep spiritual exhaustion that I felt down to the very core of my being. I just could not bear the thought of walking two miles through the darkness back to the farm. I felt like my hope was gone, that God had deserted me.

I recall walking along the edge of a canal built to guide little rivers toward the farmland. In the dark, these irrigation routes could easily be followed back to the farm. As I walked slowly back toward the village, I suddenly felt so overwhelmed with despair that I absolutely could not take another step. My whole body began to tremble, and I sank to my knees right there where I was. Great sobs racked my shaking body. I just didn't feel like being alive anymore.

*Why, God? Why have You left me here all alone?*

I looked up into the night, black as pitch, and tears streamed down my face like hot rivers.

*Where are You, God? If You can hear me, please just let me die. I can't live like this any longer. Why have You forsaken me?*

I just didn't have the strength of will to get back up on my feet to keep on walking, so I continued to cry and pray to God. I had no one else to talk to, no one who would care or even listen. The pain of missing my family was acute, and I had no one to call a friend. And so I stayed there, kneeling by the irrigation canal in the dark, pouring out my troubles to the God whom I fervently hoped was still listening.

I can't say how long I knelt there, but after some time, I heard footsteps coming toward me. When I looked up I noticed a man approaching me. It was strange to see someone else along this rural path so late in the evening. The man was dressed in simple white clothing such as a Muslim farmer might wear. He was very close to me—too close—and I knew that he had seen me. I was terrified, but I was out in the open. I knew that I couldn't hide. What would he think of me?

"Why are you crying?" The man's question was not unkind.

"I . . ." I tried to compose myself and answer as politely as I could. "I'm praying. I feel like God has abandoned me and my people."

For some reason, I just blurted out the whole truth. I guess I needed to say it to somebody, even if it was a perfect stranger. "I told God that I might as well die if things go on the way they are."

The man looked at me quizzically. "Why not go to the mosque to pray?"

I caught my breath. I wondered if I ought to just reply, "Good idea!" and let it go at that. But I didn't want to lie to the man, so I answered him directly. What did I have to lose at this point, anyway?

"I do not go to mosque," I replied. "I worship the God of Abraham, Isaac, and Jacob. I'm a Christian. He can hear me wherever I am—even out here—because my body is His temple."

I'm not sure what I expected the man in white to do or say in response to my confession. Whatever abuse he was going to give me, I just figured I would accept it along with the rest of my trials. But what he did say to me came as a complete shock.

"You have answered correctly," he responded calmly. "Don't be afraid; get up! The Lord is with you; He is closer to you than you think."

The man went on as I stared at him in disbelief. "Nothing will harm you, and the Lord will be with you wherever you go."

I was at a complete loss for words. I just stared at the man, slack jawed and motionless.

"Get up now and go," he said. I did as I was told and hurried back to my temporary home at Madame Seiko's farm. As I went, my steps felt a bit lighter and I allowed my heart to feel a new hope. Perhaps God had not forsaken me, after all.

# Chapter 14

# An Unlikely Exit

I KNEW THE TIME had come for me to resign from Madame Seiko's employ. I couldn't continue living in the openly hostile environment of the farming village. I didn't have much money, and I had no definite long-term plans, but I felt that God was prompting me to head for Alexandria. I gave my notice and left the farm immediately.

The oppressive spirit that had surrounded me in the small community faded with each mile, and my heart felt lighter. I hadn't quite realized how depressed and discouraged I had become in that place. I shuddered as I thought of how close I had come to just giving up during my time at Madame Seiko's farm. Now my hope was renewed as my mind filled with plans to find a way to get a visa to the United States. But first I needed to find a new job.

Alexandria, that marvelous ancient city, was a cosmopolitan port populated by thriving business-men from around the world. There were plenty of construction projects and a bustling commerce near the docks. I was certain to be able to find work with decent pay in such a place. Unfortunately for me, many native Egyptians were also seeking work at the docks; and they didn't like to see a foreigner find a good job. I found myself being chased away from work by Egyptians who were jealous of the English skills that earned me favor with the foreign business-men. The hostility became even more evident when they realized I was an "infidel" Christian. It was tough going, and I held several brief labor jobs until I met a fellow Sudanese Christian named Steven. He helped me find a job with a kindly developer who ran an Irish-British firm. He needed assistance wiring a high-rise building for electricity. My new employer was so generous that he paid me American dollars for my Egyptian pounds, an arrangement that was fi-nancially very favorable to me.

As I worked, I saved all the money that wasn't required for food or rent. When I wasn't working, I enjoyed hosting a Bible study in my modest apart-ment. My new friend Steven joined me, as well as men that I met from Ghana, Congo, Ethiopia, and other African nations. Life was difficult for me in Alexandria, but it was a big improvement over life in Cairo and on the farm. The diversity of the city pro-vided me with both protection and companionship.

Over time, Steven and I both had saved enough money to purchase airline tickets to the U.S. We were thrilled about the prospect of getting to freedom in America. But we soon found out that getting a visa wasn't that easy. The Americans required at least three thousand U.S. dollars over and above airfare to grant a visa. That is a tremendous amount of money for a laborer working in a third-world country to obtain. Steven and I didn't give up. We were determined to get a visa, no matter what the cost. If we couldn't get to the States, perhaps we could get a visa to France or some other western nation. So we continued to save money and visit embassies, getting nowhere fast.

One weekend, Steven and I made the trip to Cairo, again with the intention of getting a visa. Finally, we heard the bad news from the Egyptian authorities. We would not be permitted to leave Egypt without express permission from the Sudanese embassy. That was the worst news possible. The Khartoum government ran the Sudanese embassy in Cairo. There was no way they would let a couple of southern Christians like ourselves get away. We were getting more and more discouraged, and increasingly afraid of being sent back to the Sudan.

We were feeling pretty down when we headed for the train station to return to Alexandria, empty-handed once again. As we were walking through the train terminal, I felt Steven's elbow jab my ribs.

"Hey, William! Look over there!"

I followed Steven's gaze and immediately realized what he was pointing at. There was a tall white guy at a nearby queue wearing a white jacket emblazoned in English with the words, "Jesus Is Lord" on the back. We guessed that the man was an American.

"Maybe he can help us," Steven said.

I shook my head at Steven's unrealistic suggestion. "What can some tourist do to help us?" I reasoned.

"He's a Christian, isn't he? Maybe we can talk to him."

I had my doubts, and I hung behind as Steven approached the stranger.

"What's up, man?" Steven asked, with his very best imitation of American swagger. It was ludicrous —with his thick African accent, no one would ever believe he was an American. The stranger turned and took in Steven's act with a look of bemusement. I was embarrassed for Steven and for myself.

"What can I do for you guys?" the American said. He realized we were up to something, but at least he was willing to hear us out.

I quickly stepped up and we introduced ourselves. We explained that we were Christians who were trying to make it to America where we could be educated and help our families who lived under the threat of war. The stranger listened sympathetically and then extended his hand to us.

"I'm Michael Greenan, and I'll help you if I can," he offered graciously. "But just because I'm American doesn't mean I have any special influence at the U.S. embassy."

"That may be true, but they might be at least willing to listen to you," I said. "As an American, you could speak for us. They only turn us away."

Michael hesitated for a moment and then shrugged. "Okay, I'll see what I can do for you guys." He was true to his word and went with us back to the Cairo embassies. While we were there, he was an advocate for us, finally convincing the Turkish embassy to grant us a tourist visa. It happened that Michael was planning to head through Turkey himself on his way to Asia.

It was a bona fide miracle. Why a stranger would be willing to change his plans to help a couple of guys he didn't even know was beyond my understanding. Why the Turks would give us a visa was beyond all of our understanding, but it happened. Before the truth of it had even sunk in, the three of us were on a flight to Istanbul.

## "The Way of the World"

The city of Istanbul was awe-inspiring. Ancient architecture dating from the days of the Byzantines graced the skyline with delicate spires and towering domes. Crowded open-air markets were filled to overflowing with colorful goods of fine quality. The men of the city seemed to enjoy the sights as much as we were; they relaxed in the bazaars, chatting and sipping tea at a leisurely pace. Michael, Steven, and I enjoyed taking in the scenes all around us even though none of us spoke any Turkish.

Michael parted company with us after a day or two of sightseeing. He was on his way to Japan to teach English. We thanked him for his kindness and wished him well.

"I hope you guys find what you're looking for," he said as he reached into his pocket and fished out a scrap of paper, on which he hastily scribbled a note. "Here, William. If you ever make it to the States, give me a call."

I slipped the paper into my wallet and waved good-bye to the young American. I was still amazed at the way God had provided a stranger to bring me out of Egypt, and I felt in my heart that I would somehow connect with him again.

While we were in Istanbul, I spent my time trying to work toward getting a visa to the West. I wasn't seeing the results that I'd hoped for, but I didn't give up. I knew that God had a plan, as He always does. I just hadn't figured it out yet.

Soon Steven and I parted company, and I still devoted my time in Turkey to working toward a visa. When I wasn't in some government agency filling out forms, I spent my time enjoying the atmosphere of the bazaar.

One bright morning, I was sitting at the market having some tea when a young Turkish man approached me. He had heard me speaking English, and he was curious.

"Hello," he said. "May I sit here?" His words were clear and carefully pronounced, and I understood them quite readily. He introduced himself as Ahmet and explained that he would like to practice speaking English with me.

"Nice to meet you, Ahmet," I said. "My name is William. I'm glad to have someone to talk to, because I'm here by myself."

Ahmet paused for a moment, scrutinizing my

words. "You are not American or British either. Where are you from?"

"I am from Africa. I'm here on a tourist visa."

Ahmet was intrigued. It was rare to see a black man in Turkey, and he had never spoken with an African before. "William from Africa, would you like to see our museum? I can explain everything to you in English."

I was delighted to have someone to show me the museum. It was a massive series of structures from antiquity, filled with artifacts of every description. I thanked Ahmet enthusiastically.

He was a great tour guide who was obviously proud of his city and its rich culture, and rightly so. The museum was spectacular. We stopped and admired the contents of each glass-enclosed exhibit. I was amazed to see the arm of John the Baptist and the hairs of Muhammad, the prophet of Islam. I wondered how the museum had determined these strange relics to be authentic. The buildings themselves were so fabulous that my senses were overwhelmed. Artistry was evident in even the smallest corners of the elaborately tiled structures. Azure, gilt, crimson, and alabaster melted into seamless mosaics beneath sumptuous vaulted domes. Arched windows, beautifully wrought, directed thoughts heavenward as they framed the vibrant sky. Ahmet described how these buildings were transformed into mosques with the rise of the Ottoman Empire. In Byzantium, they had been Eastern Orthodox churches.

My guide admitted that he knew little of the

pre-Muslim history of Constantinople. I was able to explain to him what I knew about the history of the early church in Asia Minor, and how the churches in what is now modern-day Turkey were so important to the development of Christianity. Ahmet was surprised and pleased to find that I had learned about Turkish history even from a school in Africa. He listened politely as we continued to admire the ancient buildings.

Finally, we arrived at a display that was revered above the others. It was carefully protected, with security guards keeping watch nearby. Curious visitors leaned over velvet ropes to get a better look. The murmur of subdued voices rose above the cavernous quiet of the exhibit hall, so I knew that the crowd was excited. I wondered what artifact could generate such obvious enthusiasm.

"It is the sword of Muhammad the prophet," Ahmet whispered. "With it he conquered Mecca and prepared the world for the coming of Islam."

I was both awed and troubled by what I saw. One piece of steel, wielded by a single man, truly changed history. I felt like I was looking back through time, and the effect was dizzying. Something was bothering me, but I couldn't put my finger on the source of my unease.

I was quiet as we quit the cool of the museum for the heat of the midday sun. My new friend had shown me many wonders of the Muslim world, a counterpoint to the harsh fanaticism I had experienced in Africa. He was a man with an open mind and an open heart, and he was able to explain many of the intellectual and artistic triumphs of his culture. And yet at the end, there was the sword.

We stopped to rest over a steaming cup of tea beneath the shade of a brightly colored awning. A light breeze stirred the air and lifted the scent of the tea leaves all around us. The delicate fragrance served to calm my mind as I slowly breathed it in. I was lost in thought, trying to process the contradictions in my mind.

"What are you thinking?" Ahmet asked.

I looked up at my new friend. His eyes spoke sincerity, so I decided to trust him. "I guess I was thinking that Jesus never had a sword," I replied.

It was just a thought. I wasn't quite sure where I was headed with it. Just the same, I knew it was important.

Ahmet didn't understand what I was getting at. "Everyone carried swords in those days—that was the way of the world."

*The way of the world.* The sword has always been the way of the world. That was what my grandfather had tried to teach me so long ago at Opari. My jumbled thoughts began to make sense to me. Maybe I could explain it to Ahmet.

"A sword is the weapon of an earthly kingdom," I said. "God's kingdom *is not of this world.* That's why Jesus and Muhammad were so different."

"How do you mean? Jesus was also a great prophet, just like Muhammad."

"Jesus was different. He didn't need a sword of steel because His sword was within Himself. His sword was the Word of God. It was a different kind

of weapon, serving a different purpose." I struggled
to find the words to explain the fundamental other-
ness of Christ.

Ahmet leaned toward me, wrestling with the
dual task of understanding the English and understanding the strange new concepts he was hearing.
"How could God's words be like a sword?"

"In Islam, it is said that the Koran is the very
Word of God, brought to earth by Muhammad, is
that not so?" I tried to explain my thoughts in the
context of what I knew Ahmet believed.

"Yes, of course, I believe that," Ahmet replied.
"It is said that the word of God, the Koran, has always existed in heaven, but it was not known on
earth until it was revealed to the prophet."

"In Christianity, Jesus is called the Word of God.
It is said that the Word of God, Jesus, has always existed in heaven, but was not known on earth until
He was revealed in human form. *'In the beginning
was the Word, and the Word was with God, and the
Word was God. . . . And the Word became flesh, and
dwelt among us.'* That is from the Gospels—the *Injil*
—from the book of John."

"We accept the Injil, but I don't understand. Can
a book be God? How could a book become flesh?"
Ahmet's brow wrinkled in puzzlement. "Do you
worship a book?"

"No, we don't worship the Bible—just like you
don't worship the Koran. But the substance of the
Scripture, the Word, is part of God. We believe that
Jesus, the Word, is the same nature as God."

"Ah, but there is only one God," Ahmet mused.

"You are right. There is only one God," I told him. We certainly agreed on that point. "But Christians believe that one God exists in three persons, just like water exists in three forms. You may see steam, ice, and clear liquid, but you would call all of them equally water."

"That is true enough. But I still don't understand the part about God's Word being turned into flesh."

"This verse is speaking of Jesus," I explained. "We believe that Jesus always has existed as God— that He is the Word of God who created the universe and that He came to earth as a man. He came so that we could know God personally and be certain of our place in heaven."

Ahmet looked startled. "How can anyone know God personally? Allah does not stoop so low. And how can anyone ever be sure of his eternal destiny, unless he dies a martyr? Allah gives no guarantees but has mercy on those he pleases."

Finally I understood what had been bothering me. People always try to turn God into the ruler of an earthly kingdom, but God's plan is not about ruling the world. It is about ruling our hearts. With that sudden insight, I thought I could explain myself more clearly.

"That is the heart of the difference between our faiths," I said. "You cannot know Allah personally, and the kingdom of Islam is ruled on earth by the Shari'a—and by the sword. You have said this yourself. But the Christian concept of God is very personal. Jesus walks with us, loves us, and relates to us—and His kingdom is in heaven. He assures us of our place in that kingdom forever. You will never need an earthly weapon to defend a heavenly kingdom."

Ahmet thought about my explanation for a while before framing his reply. "I see what you are saying, but one thing in particular troubles me. You have said that you can be certain of going to heaven. What do you have to do to gain entrance to your heaven? Allah weighs our submission to the five pillars of Islam. This is an ideal way to live, and I do my best. No one can be sure if Allah will find him to be good enough, but we try."

That was an easy question for me to answer. "You are right that God weighs our submission to Himself. But God demands perfection. God says, *'Be perfect, as I am perfect.'* But no man on earth can be perfect."

"So you depend on Allah's mercy too. You never know if you are good enough."

"Yes and no," I said. "Christians depend on God's mercy. But we don't need to be good enough, because Jesus Christ was perfect. He sacrificed Himself to take the punishment that we deserved. Now when we call on Jesus, God sees only His perfection. That is how we are assured of our place in heaven."

Ahmet was silent for a time, thoughtfully draining the dregs of his teacup. "I would like to learn more about Jesus," he said.

I was dumbstruck. I was beginning to see why God had picked me up out of Egypt and dropped me down in Istanbul. His reason was Ahmet. There was no other explanation for my increasingly unbelievable odyssey.

I only saw Ahmet that one day, and the next I was off to Ankara. But on that day, Ahmet heard the gospel of Christ and believed. All I could do was direct him to the only church that existed in Istanbul at the time, an international church run by Canadians. The Lord truly works in mysterious ways.

My joy over Ahmet was real, but it was quickly overshadowed in my mind by concern for my own predicament.

## The Kindness of Strangers

When I left for Ankara, I only had ten days left on my tourist visa, and I was getting desperate. I had run out of money, and there was no church in the whole city. I found myself wandering from place to place, looking for work to tide me over for a few days.

For a foreigner, especially an African, there were few employment opportunities in Turkey. This was doubly true since I was not a Muslim. Many of the Turks made racial jokes and insults, but I ignored it. Getting angry would get me nowhere. I just needed an odd job for the cash to survive as I waited for news of a visa.

As the time on my visa grew short, it began to look as though I might end up back in Africa, facing destruction once again. As I wandered the city, I saw signs in English with directions to a military barracks. It was an *American* military barracks. I felt hope swell again in my heart. They would certainly have a chaplain there, and maybe I could get help with my visa.

I decided immediately to make a visit. I should have guessed how it might appear to the U.S. military for a Sudanese man to come rushing up to the barracks. They immediately suspected that I was up to no good. I guess I can't blame them, since Sudan has been known for harboring terrorists. Still, I was surprised when they secured me and brought me in for questioning. They were pretty suspicious of my story of searching for a chaplain until my Bible fell out of my clothing.

"Hey, I guess this guy was telling the truth," one of the officers remarked as he thumbed through the worn pages of the New Testament. "He seems harmless enough."

"He can't stay here, though," said another officer. "We don't deal with asylum cases."

I was feeling discouraged as the soldiers discussed my fate. Finally, they decided to refer me to Father Nus, a French priest. I was grateful to have someone to turn to at last.

Father Nus was kind to me, and he went out of his way to make sure I didn't end up back in the Sudan. My passport was nearly expired when he helped with arrangements for me to travel to France. He even gave me enough money for a one-way ticket to Paris.

Once again, God provided for me in a miraculous way through the kindness of a stranger. Every time things were looking impossible for me, God delivered me from circumstances beyond my control. Even so, God's provision for me through the French priest took me by surprise. After all I had been through, it was embarrassing to admit that I had been living in anxiety and fear during my stay in Turkey. I should have been trusting in God all along. Nevertheless, I was overwhelmed with gratitude and relief when I finally realized that I would finally set foot in a country where I would simply be free to be who I am: a Christian.

# Chapter 15

# America

BY THE GRACE OF GOD, I finally arrived safe and secure in the United States of America in the fall of 1988. It had been four years since I escaped from my native country of Sudan, yet I knew that my journey was just beginning. My travels now spanned four continents and three seas. I had passed the great river, I had crossed a vast desert, and I had lived as a stranger among people who were strange to me. My journey had been fraught with uncertainty and peril, but God had preserved me through it all, as though refining me by fire.

After my brief sojourn in Turkey, I spent time in Lyon, France. The French people were very kind to me, and I was permitted to remain in their country. French was language number five for me, and I studied it with a vengeance as I worked dead-end jobs to get by. I soon realized that it would take several years of study to reach a level of fluency necessary for a college education within the French university system. Still, I kept trying to advance myself. Meanwhile, I discovered that godly men like Father Nus were not all that common in the "Christian" West.

Although Europe in general and France in particular had much to offer, the post-Christian values of the French culture were quite a shock to my sensibilities. The moral codes we followed in Africa were considered to be old-fashioned by most Europeans, and many European churches were lukewarm in their enthusiasm for the gospel. Still, I managed to find a church family in France.

After nearly two years in France, God opened the door for me to travel to the United States. The opportunity was like a dream come true. As my airplane arced into the sky, I felt like my life was about to start all over again.

## New York State of Mind

I stepped out of a cab and into New York City at dawn, just as the golden rays of the sun were spreading their light across the gleaming skyline. Glass, stone, and steel glowed with dazzling brightness before the residual dusk of the wakening sky. I stood awestruck, paralyzed by the sheer magnitude of the vision before me. Though the hour was early, a sea of strangers already surrounded me. At times, I felt as though I might drown in the crushing waves of humanity rushing all around me. I had lived in busy cities like Paris, Cairo, Istanbul, and Ankara, but nothing had prepared me for these first moments in America.

As I looked around to get my bearings, I noted that I was at the Port Authority. A sign near the street corner told me that I was standing near Forty-second Street. It didn't help much to know where I was, because I had no idea where I was going. However, with only $100 in my possession, I did know that my options were limited.

A sense of panic began to overtake me as I desperately tried to think of names or phone numbers of people I had met over the years who were Americans. I must have looked as frightened and vulnerable as I felt, because as I crammed myself into a telephone booth to gather my thoughts, a pair of unsavory characters approached me, hoping to take advantage of a foreigner.

"Speak-a you ENG-lish?" one man leered, his forced smile revealing his ill-kept teeth. "Gimme ten bucks and we will help you find someplace to stay."

The first man leaned forward aggressively, smiling and reaching for my backpack. "Here, I'll carry that pack for you; just gimme ten bucks."

The second man began pressing into me, trying to remove the backpack that held my few possessions. "Please, let me help you with that."

"No, thank you," I said politely. I was unsure of how I ought to deal with these strangers who spoke like friends but felt like enemies. "I appreciate your offer, but I really don't need your help right now."

The two men refused to leave, and I didn't know

how I could extricate myself from my uncomfortable situation. As the men continued to harass me, two patrolling policemen happened by. They seemed to know immediately what was going on, because they came on over.

My tormenters beat a hasty retreat when they saw the officers.

"Hey, buddy, this is New York City," one of the cops said. "Lesson number one is 'Don't talk to strangers.'"

"Yeah, if anyone comes up to you and asks to take your luggage, don't give it to them, or you'll regret it." The second police officer paused, as if he wondered what advice he could give to someone like me—someone alone and scared in a strange country. He sighed. "If you need help, try to find a police officer. Good luck, kid."

I thanked the policemen for their assistance, and they went on their way. I was very desperate at this point, and I knew the One I really needed to call on for help was God. With my eyes open, I came before Him in silent prayer. *This is it, Lord. I don't know what to do. I'm stranded in New York City, and I don't have anywhere to go. Please help me now.*

With a renewed sense of calm, I sorted through the contents of my wallet. As I smoothed out a wrinkled old piece of paper, my heart leaped with a sudden spark of hope. Crumpled and faded, but still legible, was the address and telephone number of my friend Michael Greenan of Milton, Massachusetts. I hadn't seen Michael for nearly two years, when we had parted company back in Istanbul.

Before he left, he had handed me the phone number of his folks back in the States. He told me that if I made it to America someday, to call. Well, I had made it to America, and now that phone number had resurfaced just at the time when I needed it most. *Thank You, Lord!*

## A Friend Indeed

When I had spoken to him for the last time, Michael, the world traveler, had been headed for Japan. I had no idea whether or not he was at home or abroad. Assuming he was in the U.S., would he be living with his parents again? Would he even recall our brief friendship?

I felt awkward and unsure of myself, but I had no choice but to dial the number before me. *Please, God, let someone answer the phone. . . .*

"Hello?" a voice I did not recognize answered. "Who is this?" It was Eugene Jr., Michael's brother.

I decided to tell him my story. "You don't know me, but I am a friend of your brother Michael," I began.

My words sounded odd, even to me. I wished that I could start over, but it was too late for that. I just kept on talking. "We met in Egypt in 1986, and he said to call him if I ever ended up in the States. . . ." My voice trailed off as I considered what to say next. "I'm stranded in New York City!"

There was a pause on the other end of the line. *This guy must think I'm a lunatic,* I thought. I realized that Michael's brother had every reason to hang up on me. But he didn't.

"Uh, just a minute. My mom might be able to help you out."

A few seconds later, a new voice was on the line. "Hello? This is Kathleen, Michael's mother. How can I help you?"

I briefly explained my situation to her. I recounted my struggle to enter the U.S., and my plans to head to D.C. to seek asylum. But what I really needed was a place to stay until I could decide what steps to take. I was in New York City, and darkness was approaching fast.

There was another pause on the other end of the line as Kathleen digested the implications of my unusual and unexpected request. I could hear her consulting with her husband in the background. Finally, she returned to the line. "My son Michael is living in Phoenix now, and we will give him a call. If he can vouch for you, you are welcome in our home. Do you understand?"

I assured her that I did indeed understand, and I anxiously waited for an hour to pass before calling back. It was already getting late, and I was afraid to spend the night alone in the city with nowhere to go. I certainly had no desire to encounter more "strangers" like the ones I had met that morning. I had a feeling that the strangers would become increasingly bold and threatening under cover of darkness. I called back in precisely one hour, and Mrs. Greenan answered the phone.

"William," she said, "we spoke to Michael, and he said that he was blessed and happy to hear that you finally made it safely to the U.S. You can stay with us for as long as you have a need to."

My relief and gratitude were so great that I could barely express them. I spoke with yet another Greenan boy, Patrick, to figure out how I would get to Boston. As it turned out, I was near a Greyhound station. The $100 I had arrived with was enough to purchase a ticket on the next bus to Boston. Patrick agreed to pick me up at the bus station at 7 p.m. that evening.

"Once you get to the terminal, don't wander off. Just stay put, and I will be able to find you," he said.

I was more than happy to agree to his instructions, and I soon found myself aboard the bus bound for New England. I can still recall the wonder of that late afternoon trip. The bus wound its way through postcard-perfect scenery and quintessentially American hamlets on the four-hour trip. I took it all in with relish. If God willed, America would be my new home.

## Just Like Family

I arrived at my final destination, Boston, promptly at 7 p.m. I had no idea what Patrick would look like, so I sat down and waited. As it turned out, I could tell when I saw him that Patrick was Michael's brother, and he was genuinely glad to meet me. I was so warmly received by the Greenan family that I felt as though I was an old family friend instead of a foreigner and a perfect stranger.

Over a hearty meal, they plied me with questions about my life back in Sudan, my family, and my long journey to the States.

Soon the phone rang. It was Michael calling to welcome me. "Jesus is Lord, brother!"

"Amen to that," I replied. I told him the whole story from where we had left off, and we reminisced about our days in Egypt and our journey to Turkey. It was then that we both realized that our friend Steven hadn't made it. We prayed for Steven and asked God to protect him, wherever he might be. We gave thanks to God for bringing me safely to the United States. Then we turned our attention to practical matters.

"Look, William, I would love to get together with you," Michael said, "but that won't happen for a while. I'm headed out again—this time to southern Africa. Do you have any type of visa or green card?"

I told him that I didn't.

"Okay, you will have to get some sort of permit before you can get a job."

"Yes, I know a little about how that works. I am hoping to get some paperwork when I apply for asylum. That is why I plan to head for Washington, D.C., next."

Michael paused for a moment. "Hmmm . . . it won't be easy for you to get by before you get that taken care of. I'll tell you what; I'll wire you some money to help you until you can get on your feet."

Michael was true to his word and added kindness to kindness by assisting me financially. The Greenans proved to be amiable hosts, giving me a quiet room with a bed on the third floor of their home. Eugene and Kathleen Greenan could relate to my story as an immigrant, because they were both immigrants themselves. They had been raised in Ireland before venturing to America in their youth. In America they met, married, and raised six children before retiring and becoming happy grandparents. But they loved to keep alive the memory of their old home in Ireland. I was inspired and encouraged by their story.

On Sunday, they invited me along to the local Catholic church in town, where we had a wonderful time and I enjoyed the fellowship of brothers and sisters in Christ. Everyone was so warm and receptive that I felt right at home. During the two weeks that I spent with the Greenan family, I spent a lot of time talking with Patrick. He and I shared a lot of common goals and interests, and he was studying engineering at Northeastern University in Boston.

I wanted to go to school desperately, so that I would be in a position to help my family and my country. But I didn't know where to start. I knew I had lost four years of schooling since leaving high school in 1984. I would have been a senior in college if not for my need to flee the country. Patrick understood how I felt and was a big encouragement to me.

"American schools are no more difficult than any other schools," he said. "Besides, foreign students always seem to do well if they study hard. You are fluent in French and English, and your science skills are strong, so you should do fine."

"How do I get into an American college?" I asked.

"Well, I know they have student visas for foreign students, but you would still need money for tuition, and you would need your high school records."

Unfortunately, those were three things I did not have. I was beginning to understand the obstacles I would face, but I was determined to remain undeterred. I knew I couldn't depend on the Greenans' hospitality indefinitely, yet I literally had no resources. Eugene Jr. and Patrick were resuming their studies as college was starting up again. I knew I needed God's help and direction. I prayed and cried out to God for an hour without stopping, and then I was quiet. I listened for God's plan as I searched my heart. Finally, I came to a decision.

My plan was simple. I purchased a round-trip bus ticket to Washington, D.C., as a sort of insurance policy. I felt that if a job opportunity did not present itself in D.C., I could always return to New England to work while I waited for asylum to be approved.

So, I said good-bye to my gracious hosts and headed for the U.S. capital with nothing but a Bible and the clothes on my back. Little did I know, my life was about to take another unexpected turn.

## A Pilgrim in Newark

While I was on the bus, I fell into a sound sleep. When I awoke, the bus was in the station. I was a bit groggy, but I disembarked and went to gather my wits about me and decide how I ought to apply for asylum. As it turned out, my journey had only taken me to Newark, New Jersey. I just assumed that the bus had reached D.C., when in fact it had only stopped briefly to board new passengers.

When I inquired at the ticket counter, I was shocked to discover that Washington was still 230 miles away and the bus was already long gone. I suppose I could have returned the following day to claim a seat on the next bus, but I didn't. I remembered the stories I had learned in school about the colonists in the New World. The pilgrims had landed at Plymouth Rock, and then they settled nearby. I decided that I, like the pilgrims before me, would just settle where I landed. And I had just landed in Newark.

Actually, my decision was helped along a bit by the local police. It was illegal to stay in the bus station past midnight, so they suggested that I move along. One of them mentioned that I might try to find the local YMCA if I needed a place to stay.

I finally arrived at the Newark Y at around one in the morning. I was tired but hopeful. At the desk, a security guard leaned back and eyed me suspiciously. "What do you want?"

"I need a place to stay, please," I said. "I have nowhere to go."

"Nope." The guard looked bored, but a hint of a smile played at the edge of his lips, as though he enjoyed the prospect of turning me away. "Got to fill in a form, and it'll take about a week for a room to open up for you. Go on; you can get a form tomorrow."

I edged toward a chair and tried to sit down.

"Go on, get out of here, I said." The guard was getting angry. "You can't loiter here in the lobby."

I persisted and continued to stand in the lobby. We argued for some time, and we were still at it by 5 a.m., when a young guy came down the elevator. He overheard our argument and wandered over to check out the action.

"Hey, are you from Africa?"

"Yes, I need someplace to stay, just for the day."

He looked me over for a minute, and then came up with a proposition. "Hey, I'm headed out for the day, and I need five bucks. If you give me five, you can stay in my room until I get back."

The guard nodded his assent, and the deal was made.

I woke up at midmorning and headed to Congressman Peter Rodino's office. I was able to speak with his secretary and explain my situation. Mr. Rodino's secretary was very kind to me. She wrote me a nice letter on behalf of the congressman, who was in D.C. at the time. With the benefit of her letter, I was entitled to get some help from Newark Christian charity organizations and churches. She specifically suggested that I should see Pastor Charles Brown and Bishop Lukas on Broad Street. She told me that they helped homeless people who needed shelter.

After I left the congressman's office, I headed to the office of the Immigration and Naturalization Service. I admitted that I was an unregistered alien, and I explained that the Government of Sudan was interested in ending my life. I was sure they believed my story, because they immediately sent me to the FBI office in Jersey City. They even put me on the Path (Port Authority Trans-Hudson) Train for free. I was so excited that I was going to see the FBI. I didn't know what it was, but I was still excited and happy.

When I arrived at the FBI, two armed agents in civilian clothes came to greet me. I handed them the papers that the INS had given me and looked to them expectantly. I was sure that these special government agents would grant my asylum. I soon realized, however, that the FBI was not in the asylum business. In fact, I was led to a room to be interrogated.

They asked me countless questions about the Government of Sudan and about spying and about communism. I answered everything to the best of my ability. Eventually, the agents were satisfied that I was not a dangerous spy. They handed me a new set of papers and sent me on my way.

By the time I got back to Newark, it was once again getting late in the day. I still was without legal papers to work in the U.S., and I was running out of money fast. I knew I didn't have enough money to stay at the YMCA, even if a room were available. So I took the advice given to me by the congressman's secretary and headed for Broad Street. I found the Reverend Brown's office and gave him the note from Mr. Rodino's office.

Reverend Brown was kind to me and gave me food and shelter for the night. I had no problem following the rules and going to church services as their shelter policy required. I soon discovered that many of the homeless people that Reverend Brown and Bishop Lukas helped were plagued by problems such as drugs, alcohol, violence, and prostitution. These men of God helped with the physical as well as the spiritual needs of all these people without discrimination.

The two preachers allowed me to stay at the shelter until I received asylum applications and a work permit from the INS, and then they approached me with an unusual offer. They knew that I was different from many of the young men at the shelter, and that I was a brother in Christ. Bishop Lukas pastored a church downtown that had once been a Jewish synagogue. The Jewish congregation had abandoned the building permanently after the riots of 1964. There was an empty room in the basement, and Bishop Lukas asked me if I would like to stay in the church rather than in the crowded homeless shelter.

I accepted immediately—I was thrilled with his kind offer. *God must have a sense of humor,* I thought. *This old church still has a star of David on it!* God didn't want me to forget my Hebrew roots as I settled into my new Christian life in America. What a comfort He is to His people. God also must understand irony, because Reverend Brown soon approached me with an unlikely job offer.

## Y-Shaped Mission Field

"William, good news," Reverend Brown said to me. "I found a job for you."

I assured him I was willing to take any job, any job at all.

"Listen, William, this is an election year in our country. The vice president, George H. W. Bush, is running against the governor of Massachusetts, Michael Dukakis. They need people to run the 'Get Out the Vote' campaign. The job only lasts one month, but you will have money until you can find a permanent job."

Reverend Brown took me to the campaign offices, and I was hired on the spot. The wage was $100 per week, which was a lot of money to me. My job was to take registration forms and approach people to sign up to vote.

For one month I pounded the pavement, asking strangers to sign up to vote. People scorned me, saying that I was obviously a foreigner who didn't realize that the government didn't care about their needs. I encouraged them not to take their freedom for granted. I told them that in Sudan, we have no freedom at all and no right to vote for anyone.

It was my great desire to be a citizen of America with the right to vote. Of course, as an unregistered alien, I couldn't. Still, I did manage to convince some Americans to do so. I also had the opportunity to meet some political candidates, such as Donald Payne and Frank Lautenberg, who would later prove to be helpful in the advancement of my asylum case and educational needs.

On November 8, 1988, Election Day came. Vice President Bush won handily, and my job was over. Armed with a new Social Security document and official working papers, I decided to network among my Christian friends.

The Reverend Glen Hatfield was a brother whom I connected with right away. He was the pastor of the First Baptist Peddie Memorial Church. His church was also downtown, located near the YMCA. He extended me an invitation to worship at his church and suggested that I might find work through the Catholic Relief Agency.

Things began to fall in place quickly for me. I got a job at Nurser Alloy Electrical Wire on the second shift, providing me with enough money to rent my own room at the YMCA. I thanked Reverend Brown and Bishop Lukas for their gracious support and for the care I had received at the homeless shelter mission. They were blessed to hear that I had found steady work and was now able to provide for myself.

I rented a single room at the YMCA and began to attend Peddie Memorial Church. The Y was a convenient place to live because of its proximity to transportation, libraries, and government offices that I needed to visit. It was also affordable for me.

Unfortunately, the YMCA had some problems that I was not aware of. I found out that the Y was known for all kinds of problems, including drug dealers, homosexuality, violence, and alcoholism. In fact, these problems were rampant at the Newark Y.

At first, I was terrified to live with the kind of people who I discovered were living all around me. I had never been around such people, and I feared that I might be robbed, attacked, or even killed. But God spoke to my heart through His Word: *I can do all things through Christ, who strengthens me.*

I knew that God was with me and that He would

keep me safe in His will. He taught me to love instead of fear my neighbors. As God emboldened me, I decided to become a part of the solution. I began to invite everyone I met at the YMCA to come to church and to seek God in his life. I shared my testimony with them. I challenged them to stay away from drugs and to keep sober. Some of the men I spoke with began to attend church, and their lives were transformed.

## Educational Challenges

Although God provided for me with a steady job and a place to live, I knew that I had to eventually get back to school if I had any hope of helping my family. One day I went to visit the campus of Essex County College with a friend from Nigeria who was a student there. He was very encouraging and sympathetic as I told him of my desire to attend college.

"Do you have a high school diploma?" he asked.

"Yes, I have one," I replied. "I sat for the London-based Ordinary Level General Certificate back in Juba, but when I fled the country I did not stop to get a copy."

"Could you write for it?"

"Unfortunately, the high school I attended was Catholic, and all the non-Muslim schools were closed indefinitely due to war." I shuddered as I imagined what my old classrooms must look like now—empty or bombed-out shells. "Anyway, I know I can't go to college without a diploma!"

"That isn't always true, William," he said.

"Have you ever heard of the GED?"

He explained to me that GED stands for "General Equivalent Diploma" and that it is given six times per year.

"If you're ready, you could sign up and take it tomorrow," he said. "If not, buy a study guide and take it the next time around."

My heart was revived by new hope after I learned of the GED. The very next day I purchased a study guide and began an intensive plan of study. I studied all day, worked the evening shift, and then studied all day on Saturdays. On Sundays, I worshiped at Peddie Memorial.

Finally, six weeks later, I sat for the GED and received a high score. Reverend Hatfield was excited by the result, and he assured me that I would have full access to American colleges.

I immediately applied to Essex County College for the spring semester, but there were challenges that weighed heavily on my mind. I did not have a student visa, so I could not qualify for any type of student loan. The only advantages I had were a student discount at the YMCA and a legal work permit. I had to continue to work full time, and I could only afford eight credits that first semester. I managed to take two more classes during the summer session, giving me a total of thirteen credits with a 3.9 grade point average. I knew that I needed to work full time, but I also wanted to attend school full time. I had to seek God's will once again.

God gave me the idea to quit my second-shift job at Nurser Alloy and take a full-time job as a night-shift security officer. That would enable me to take a full-time schedule of classes while still working. The only problem with the arrangement was that there was no time for sleep. But I knew that God would sustain me, and indeed He did.

The night watchman job was at a filthy garbage dump. My duties involved hourly patrols of the facilities and granting access to garbage truck drivers. I had a small office with a monitor screen and a coffeepot. The tiny space was quiet, and it was an ideal place for studying when I wasn't patrolling the grounds. My studies were helpful to keep me awake and alert on the job. Sometimes fellow students would show up at my little booth at the dump to ask for my help. I was always willing to help other students who needed assistance. And to be honest, I appreciated their company. Having a visitor at the job helped me to stay awake, which was not always easy with only three hours of sleep every twenty-four hours.

During the day, I learned to "power nap" between classes to keep my strength up. The brief naps kept my mind clear enough to absorb lectures about calculus, physics, chemistry, and engineering. Miraculously, I remained healthy and was able to maintain a 3.5 GPA with fifteen credits in my major of Computer Integrated Manufacturing Engineering that semester.

With that hurdle under my belt, I applied for an academic scholarship, the Essex County College Presidential Scholarship. I won the scholarship, which paid full tuition for the next semester. In fact,

I won that scholarship each semester for the two years I took to complete Essex College. I graduated with high honors and an associate's degree in Computer Integrated Manufacturing Engineering.

And so, the year of 1989 ended on a good note. I did well in college. I had a job, a church home at Peddie Memorial, and a room at the YMCA. God was taking care of me, as usual.

# Chapter 16

# Higher Education

I GRADUATED FROM Essex County College in the fall of 1990, and the following spring I was able to enroll as a junior at New Jersey Institute of Technology (NJIT). I signed up for a schedule to suit my engineering major, but I soon found out that I had unwittingly enrolled in "Human Relationships 101." Science and technology were so logical and easy for me to understand, but understanding other people was not always so straightforward. I guess that I had been sheltered during my first two years in the United States, because I had surrounded myself with fellow Christians. The Americans I knew were people like the Reverend Hatfield and the Greenan clan. These people treated me like family, encouraging me and caring for me freely. For me, there was always a welcome. Perhaps that is why I was taken off guard by the depth of bitterness and racial division that I encountered on campus.

I moved out of the YMCA and into the NJIT dormitories, expecting to find an exciting academic environment with debates framed around great ideas and opposing worldviews. What I found was something a bit less lofty—racism. My roommate, Devon, had been deeply affected by racism throughout his life. There was anger and hurt just below the surface, always ready to spill over. His rage expressed itself outwardly in the form of hatred for white people, in general, and for our next-door neighbors, in particular.

When I moved in, Devon and our neighbors in the dorm were already engaged in hostilities. I can't say who started it, but by then it didn't really matter. The Caucasian boys next door taunted Devon with offensive comments, and he responded in kind. The situation escalated daily, and every morning when I returned from my shift as a night watchman, I heard about the latest skirmish. For all of Devon's bluster, I could tell that he felt demoralized by the situation. His confidence in himself was shaken. I hoped that the student housing authorities would deal with the problem, but they didn't seem to care. I guess they believed the old saying, "Sticks and stones may break my bones, but words will never hurt me." Well, words can hurt. And for people who don't have Jesus to turn to, the pain can turn into a deep well of bitterness.

## Understanding Devon

One morning I returned from work to find Devon agitated and obviously angry. His expression was hard as he paced the floor of the small space that we shared.

"What's up, Devon?" I asked politely. To tell the truth, I had a pretty good idea of what his answer was going to be. I didn't really want my day to start out with more disturbing news, but I figured he needed to talk.

"Those white boys, that is what's up," Devon spat back, emphasizing his words with a punch of his fist in their general direction. "They said I would never earn my degree. They said I was stupid, just like all the brothers." Devon took a deep breath, drawing air with a hiss through his clenched teeth. "They told me to give it up and learn to play basketball."

As Devon's words hung in the air, I was stunned into silence. The insults were so demeaning that I wasn't sure what to say. I did know that I needed to say something that would help my roommate feel better.

"Devon," I began, "you and I both know that you have what it takes to succeed. Those boys know it too. They're just looking for trouble. They want you to feel angry, and they want you to react. Don't give them the satisfaction." I was trying to use reason to diffuse a volatile emotion, but it wasn't working too well. "Be the better man, and let those words pass. They don't even deserve your time."

I knew right away that my pep talk had fallen on deaf ears. I had spoken in platitudes, but he needed to hear something more practical. Devon had already dealt with more than he could take, and he was losing control.

"What do you know, William? What do you really know about white oppression?" Devon turned to face me, his eyes dark with rage. He was tall and imposing, and he leaned close to me as his voice rose in volume. "You're an African! You think you know it all, but you don't know *nothin'* about what it means to be oppressed."

My roommate was breathing hard. I wanted to tell him to calm down, but I held my tongue. I figured I was about to get an earful, and I was right.

"You have no idea what it is like to be hated for who you are! You have never been a slave in the white man's world—you have no right to tell me anything!"

I was unable to respond as Devon unleashed his verbal attack against me. I felt confused and even intimidated—there was no reason for him to accuse me. While it was true that I had not experienced white-on-black racism during my life, I did know a thing or two about oppression. I doubted that Devon had ever been arrested, tortured, or forced to live in exile. I was pretty sure that his family was not starving in a refugee camp. He was probably unaware that actual chattel slavery was still a reality back in the Sudan. But I just kept my mouth shut as Devon continued his tirade.

"You Africans think you are so superior, but you

are just fools. You think you can be equal with whites with your college education and your shirt and tie. You are wrong! They will make you a slave again."

Devon strode over to his side of the dorm room and pointed to a poster of his hero, Malcolm X. "Malcolm understood," he continued. "The Nation of Islam understands. We don't need your white men. We need a revolution! That is what you can't understand."

Devon felt that I couldn't understand him because I was an African, raised where dark skin color was the norm. I had enjoyed status as a member of a racial majority. No one had ever looked at me and then looked away because I was black. Similarly, I felt that Devon couldn't understand me because he was raised in freedom, far away from tribal warfare and religious persecution. He never had to run away from his own country. Nobody had ever hunted him down because of his beliefs. How could I communicate to him that the best weapon to fight oppression is God's Word?

"Look, Devon, all that the Nation of Islam understands is hate. And hate breeds more hate. It numbs the pain for a while, like a drug, but in the end it destroys everyone. God is the One who understands. He knows what you are going through, and He can heal you. Jesus teaches us to love our enemies, even though we may have reasons to hate them. That brings healing to everybody.

"Take Dr. Martin Luther King, for example," I continued. "He knew what racism was all about. In his day, it was a lot worse than it is now. He was able to overcome evil with good, like it says in the Bible."

As I spoke to Devon, I was also speaking to myself. I had to depend on God daily to love my own enemies. I knew that if I harbored hatred toward the jihadists, it would destroy my own spirit and ruin my Christian testimony.

Devon had every reason to feel angry, and I sensed that my words sounded empty to his ears. I just felt that he needed hope and confidence. Then I was reminded of the book of James, chapter two: *If I see a man naked and hungry, and I say to him, "Be warmed and filled" and yet do not reach out to help him, what good is it?*

How could I watch this freshman student struggle with calculus and physics—not to mention life—and yet do nothing to help? I knew what I had to do.

"Devon," I ventured, "since I'm a junior, I have already taken all of your classes. I can help you work through the assignments. You will prove those boys are wrong about you when you get the grade. They'll have to eat their words."

I was faithful to my promise to Devon, even though it was hard for me. I was so tired after my night shift, and then I had to start the day with an overload of my own classes. But I understood that God was calling me to serve my roommate and to be a witness for Him in Devon's life.

## Lessons in Division—and Unity

God was faithful to me, as well. Through my involvement with InterVarsity Christian Fellowship (IVCF), I developed a great network of supportive Christian friends. I met students from around the globe, representing many cultures and several nations. My friends from IVCF buoyed my spirit and helped me maintain perspective. What a contrast there was between the unity of believers and the divisions and racial tension that gripped the rest of the campus. Every morning when I returned from work, I spent an hour in Bible study and prayer back in the dorm room.

I invited Devon to study the Bible with me, and I was surprised when he agreed. It turned out that although Devon admired Malcolm X and the Nation of Islam, he was not a Muslim himself. He wasn't particularly religious at all, but he was willing to listen to what I had to say.

I shared verses of love from God's Word. I told my roommate that God loved him personally. I explained that we are to love God with all of our hearts, minds, and strength—and love our neighbor as ourselves.

"Those students who live next door are not just 'white people'; they are God's creation, just like you and me," I told him. "Jesus died for them and for us too. He wants all of us to turn from our sins and be saved. In Christ, all men become brothers."

Devon glared at me. He hadn't seen much Christian brotherhood in American churches. "How can you be a Christian and love white people when you know that they used Christianity to justify slavery?"

"Evil men have used God to justify their own evil deeds since time began. Ever since Cain killed Abel, Satan has been at work spreading hate and division between brothers. Real Christians do not use their faith as an excuse to sin. The Bible condemns oppression, cruelty, and hatred in the strongest terms."

Devon made no reply, giving me the opportunity to elaborate. I flipped through the Gospels, pointing out some of the statements that Jesus had made. "If you practice sin, you are a slave to sin. Hatred is bondage just as surely as chains. But Jesus is the Truth, and the Truth will set you free." Then I turned to Isaiah for a picture of the suffering servant. "Jesus Himself never tried to rule over anybody. He said that the greatest of His followers were those who served others, not enslaved them."

"Okay, so those slave master Christians were hypocrites. Big deal. What do you expect from those people? Forget it. We don't need their religion anyway. Let the white folk have their religion; we have our own."

"If you think that Christianity is the white man's religion, you are very wrong." I was adamant about this point. Too many people wanted to portray Africa as a land of godless heathens with Islam as the only monotheistic tradition there. Nothing could be further from the truth. The Hebrew traditions as well as the very earliest Christian traditions were cradled in Africa.

"If you read your history, you will know that it

was African missionaries who helped spread the gospel in Europe while white men were still pagans and barbarians," I said. "You might also find that the Irish made pilgrimages to Africa to learn how to be monks. Jesus wasn't exactly a Westerner either. He happened to choose to come to earth as a Middle-Eastern Jew. He spent His early years in Africa, where His people had been kept as slaves. The first churches outside of Jerusalem were in Asia Minor. Jesus died for the sins of the whole world. Christianity is a faith for all peoples, of every race—it doesn't matter if you are black, white, yellow, or brown."

Devon didn't reply. I wondered what he was thinking. There were deep wounds in Devon's heart, and I figured there was more to it than just a few racist remarks by the students next door. I didn't know what hate and rejection he had experienced, but I did know that more hate and rejection was not the answer. Only the love and forgiveness of Christ could give Devon peace of mind and a sense of personal worth. I prayed that he would find that peace someday.

One thing was certain, and that was that Devon did not find peace that first semester at NJIT. His grades slipped as he became increasingly bitter and angry. One day I returned home to the dorm room to find that Devon was gone. He had overturned my bed and my books—the dorm room was a mess. He had written a vicious note and taped it to the door of our neighbors in the dormitory.

I felt hurt that he had taken out his rage on me, but more than that I felt a deep sense of sadness for

Devon. I could clean up my room, but would Devon be able to pick up the pieces of his life? I hoped so.

I didn't know whether Devon would be returning in the fall, but for the summer anyway, I was alone in my room. I decided to take summer classes so that I could advance more quickly.

## A Full Load

I figured it would be lonely on campus with so many of my friends leaving for summer vacation, but soon God allowed me to cross paths with a northern Sudanese student named Karim. I had heard about him earlier in the spring, but I had hesitated to look him up because I had assumed he would be a northern Muslim who would be hostile toward me. For a whole semester I had kept my distance, but given the circumstance I couldn't avoid speaking with him any longer. During the course of our conversation, it came up that he was a Sudanese Christian of Egyptian descent, not an Arab. I was embarrassed to realize that my own prejudice toward northern Sudanese people had kept me from reaching out to him. He was only eighteen, and he was unaware of the depth and severity of the war, which was taking place mainly in the South.

I briefly described some of the problems that were occurring in the Sudan, and I suggested that we should get together after he returned from summer vacation. Even though we had only just met, we took a moment to pray for each other and for our families back home. As he turned to go, I told him that if for any reason he should decide not to return to the Sudan, he would be welcome to room with me for the summer. He thanked me and then left.

Two days later, I received a phone call at the dormitory. It was Karim, and his voice was trembling.

"William, I may take you up on your offer. I need a place to stay."

"Of course, Karim, you are welcome," I replied. "What happened?" It sounded like he had been crying.

"I can't go home. It is too dangerous for me. My father . . . " His voice broke. "My father was falsely accused of violating Islamic law. He didn't do anything! The Islamic regime is after him because he is not a Muslim."

"Is he safe?"

"I don't know. They confiscated his business and took all of our money."

Worse yet, Karim informed me that his mother had been diagnosed with a brain tumor and was sent to Holland for treatment. "I have no place to go," he told me.

"Don't worry, Karim," I said. "You can stay with me. We will trust God to carry your mom through her treatment and keep your dad safe."

Karim moved in with me right away, and we supported each other. Knowing my new roommate, a northern Sudanese, helped to open my eyes to the persecution faced by Christians everywhere. It wasn't only the South Sudanese people who suffered. There were persecuted Christians in every country dominated by Islam.

We opened our dorm room for InterVarsity small group Bible studies, which we led together. I continued to work full time and maintained a schedule of two classes. I also continued to participate in cross-country races. Karim found a summer job with one of the professors. We prayed every day for a miracle for Karim. I felt his burden, and it became my own. Although we were constantly busy with work, studies, and InterVarsity activities, I could tell that Karim was constantly thinking about his family, especially his mother.

In August, Karim got his miracle. His mother, Dr. Grace, arrived in the United States. The doctors in Holland were able to remove the growth in her brain, and she was regaining her vision! Originally, the surgeon had told Dr. Grace that she would lose her sight when the tumor was removed, because of the precarious location of the mass. Miraculously, she was spared from that outcome. I was rejoicing with Karim, because I had begun to regard him as a younger brother during our brief time together. God was merciful to Grace, and granted her healing and a reunion with her son. Even so, things were still going to be very difficult for Karim's family. Grace was unable to return to the Sudan, and there was no longer any way for the family to earn a living due to the confiscation of their business and all of their foreign currency.

As it turned out, Dr. Grace was stranded at NJIT with nowhere to go. So, as Karim had become my brother, Grace became my mother. I offered her my room to sleep in since I was at work during the night shift. This arrangement worked out well for all of us.

We got along well together, like a real family. Grace's presence on campus seemed to strike a chord in the hearts of other foreign students who, for various reasons, were unable to return home. These students from places like China, Ghana, Ecuador, and Santa Lucia seemed to gain strength and comfort from Karim's mother. Our little family unit was a small reminder of the homes that they missed so much. More than that, it was an opportunity for us to minister to students from around the world with the gospel message. The love that we shared was tangible evidence of the faith that had brought us together.

The years I spent in college were incredibly full. I am still amazed that God preserved my health and gave me the ability to succeed with almost no sleep at all. I threw myself into my relationships with the same vigor that I threw myself into my studies, and both blessed me. During those vital, formative years, my professors gave me a wonderful college education. But my higher education came from the Lord.

Note: *In this chapter, I use the word "race" to describe human diversity. This is simply a matter of convention, because it is a commonly used term. I believe that there is only one "race," and that is the human race. Skin color and cultural values are superficial differences. It is my firm opinion that if ethnic differences did not exist, people would find some other reason to hate one another!*

# Chapter 17

# Operation Nehemiah

THE SUMMER OF 1993 was a major turning point in my life. I had just graduated from NJIT, and my future was bright. There was one last retreat that I planned to attend with fellow students from Inter-Varsity Christian Fellowship, only now as an alumnus. The IVCF students had become like a family to me, and I knew I would be missing them as we all went on our separate paths.

It was a great feeling to head to Camp Pinnacle, near Albany, New York. Spring was in full bloom, and the optimism of the season seemed to fit my mood. I was ready for a time of spiritual renewal and direction, as I would soon be heading into a great new career.

The theme of the section I had chosen to participate in at the retreat was "Christ and Culture." This topic was of special interest to me, because I had experienced such vastly diverse cultures in my journey. Through each culture and each community, the body of Christ was generally an example of a unifying spirit that was uniquely able to transcend ethnic barriers. Even so, I had also witnessed divisions that were all too similar to those found in the world of unbelievers. As a Sudanese national and a messianic Jew, and now as an adopted American, I was already straddling some pretty divergent cultures. For that reason, I was more acutely aware of the challenges faced by the church today with respect to cultural diversity, racism, and ethnic strife. I wanted to be prepared to serve the community as a Christian leader as I entered the "real world" in my new culture. I wanted to understand how Christ and Christianity could interact with the culture and transform it for the glory of God.

Scott Davis, my roommate and college pastor, was leading the group meeting. I felt a heavy burden in my spirit as we discussed our responsibilities and roles as new graduates entering the workforce. I prayed earnestly throughout each session and continually grilled my teachers with questions. I just couldn't shake the feeling that God was trying to tell me something—but what?

After several rounds of pretty intense class work, the whole group got together for a special prayer meeting for the persecuted believers in the Sudan. Karim and Rami, brothers from northern Sudan, and I had a special heart for this topic. We felt led to hold this special prayer session. I thought perhaps that the heaviness I felt in my spirit was a prompting, an urging of the Holy Spirit to enter into prayer for my fellow Sudanese. Even so, after our time of heartfelt intercession, the burden persisted. I knew that God was at work. I really felt as though God was getting ready to do something big. I just didn't understand that God wanted to do something big *in my life.*

## Receiving My Call

As the IVCF conference was drawing to a close, the staff called all of the Christ in Culture section students together for a special time of prayer. A number of the students in this section had received a call into full-time ministry. Some were planning to serve in the inner city; some were planning to serve around the world. The training they had received was sure to help them to adjust to their new lives in foreign lands or within an ethnic group that was different from their own. The staff called those particular students forward so that the rest of the students could pray over them and intercede for their calling. I drew close in order to pray for the students heading into ministry.

"William." I looked up and noticed that Scott was motioning to me. "Go and sit with the students in the circle."

"But I'm not going into the ministry," I whispered. "I'm an engineer."

"I think you have been called to serve," he insisted. Some of the other students nearby heard our hushed exchange and began to encourage me. "Yes, William, go on!"

"We ought to pray for you; I feel it."

I didn't feel prepared. I didn't feel adequate. I felt awkward, and unsure of myself. But still, there was a sense of rightness in my spirit as the sense of heaviness gave way to a sense of purpose.

*God, is this what You have been trying to tell me?*

I made my way into the circle and sat down with the other students who had been called to serve. As a multitude of hands stretched out over me, I felt God's power and confirmation that there was indeed a calling in my life. I still had no idea what that calling might be.

We returned home from the retreat on May 22. Two days later, I received a visit from Matt Simon, the assistant pastor of the Beth Israel Messianic Center, which had become my home church. The church's district leader for the New Jersey area was retiring, and they wanted me to replace him. After some nervous reluctance and much prayer, I agreed to fill the position.

As I served the members of Beth Israel, I could feel myself being transformed into a servant of Christ. Even though my grandfather and my father had been spiritual leaders in their communities, I had never in my life felt any desire to follow in their footsteps. I was prepared to be a fine layman and church member, but never a full-time minister. The future I had envisioned for myself involved material success. Pastors don't climb the corporate ladder. I believed that I could help my family most by earning money to support them. But God already had other plans in mind, and He was shaping me and molding me into the person that He wanted me to be.

In June my cousin Rev. John Moi and his family were in town to visit with some friends from Grace Presbyterian Church in Montclair, New Jersey. I was glad to have a chance to fellowship with him again, so I invited him to Beth Israel to hear a special speaker. He was happy to accompany me. The special speaker was Richard Wurmbrand, founder of Voice of the Martyrs, a group dedicated to helping persecuted Christians around the world. He and his wife, Sabina, had come to my church to talk about the situation in Sudan.

That weekend, God used the Wurmbrands to prepare the hearts of the congregation to respond to the plight of the persecuted church in the Sudan. As John and I listened to Pastor Wurmbrand explain in detail the horrors of persecution in the southern regions of our homeland, our spirits were challenged and convicted.

My heart was broken for my people. I could see my father's face in my mind's eye. He was a precious, loving man whom, I learned had been murdered in 1987 for his faith. I could picture my mother and sisters running for their lives, with eyes blinded by tears. How long could they survive the privations of the refugee camps? I no longer knew what I ought to pray, but I offered my weakness and my anguish up to my heavenly Father. I realized that the seed that God had planted in my heart was beginning to take root and grow.

## A Vision for Sudan

I knew that God had put my cousin and me together at just the right time in both of our lives to hear Richard Wurmbrand's message. The pleas to help our brothers and sisters in Sudan seemed to be coming directly from the Holy Spirit, speaking to me and to John.

We could not say no. The following evening, I made arrangements to visit with the Wurmbrands at the home of some of their Romanian friends in the next town on their itinerary, Cedar Grove, New Jersey. Richard had been extremely encouraging to me when I mentioned my vision to help the Sudanese people, and now I sought his advice. The Wurmbrands and their friends warmly welcomed me, as well as Karim and several InterVarsity students. Meeting with Richard and Sabina was like meeting with real saints of modern-day Christianity. They encouraged us to go forward with God to change the situation in the Sudan for all of the Christians there. We discussed several possible options, and Pastor Wurmbrand gave me thoughtful advice.

That evening, in June of 1993, I became sure of my calling. A vision to hold a prayer vigil at the United Nations as a way to draw attention to the plight of the South Sudanese people began to form in my mind. And I finally understood that if anything were to be done for my people, I would have to put my very life on the line. I decided to relinquish my worldly ambition and allow God to do His work through me. That night, I returned home to Newark a changed man.

The next few days brought a flurry of activity and phone calls as I sought help from friends and Sudanese nationals in exile. Within days, a meeting was arranged in New York City at the home of the Reverend Elioba Lado. A large group of exiled Christians from the South Sudan were mobilized to discuss the troubles of our people back home. I was energized by the belief that we would all be of one mind and one accord in our desire to help our brothers.

God knew that I would need bountiful prayers and encouragement to see this vision through, and the leadership of Beth Israel wasted no time in their wholehearted agreement to help. Soon momentum began to build.

Looking back, I am still amazed at the way God orchestrated circumstances to make it possible for His will to be accomplished through me. I am even more amazed when I realize that He had to break my will to conform to His at almost every step. But of course, nothing is impossible with God!

Because of the Christ in Culture retreat, I was prepared to minister among people who were not of my cultural background. Because of my willingness to work with the people of Beth Israel, I gained the trust and support of an entire congregation. Because of a visit from Pastor Wurmbrand, the hearts of that congregation were prepared to minister to Sudan, and I was given a vision. Because my cousin John happened to be in town, he also felt the vision. None of this was my own doing. Only God deals the cards like that.

I was blessed by the enthusiastic support of my church. Gary Selman, a pastor, and Paul Liben, a writer and historian, took the lead in helping me to get things done. Gary was also a radio man, one of two "Nice Jewish Boys" on a local station. He and Rabbi Jonathan broadcast a gospel program every Wednesday, and they brought me on the air several times to share my testimony. They also introduced me to Andy Anderson, a brother who broadcast the gospel from another local station. Paul Liben assisted me by writing professional articles for the print media and getting in touch with local news venues. The women of the congregation helped in so many practical ways. Jan Selman made a beautiful box to collect donations to offset expenses. Wonderful sisters designed and created banners and everything that was needed for the march at the UN.

The first seed money for the project was a small sum donated by a poor woman who lived on disability. Her generosity reminded me of the widow in the Bible who gave all that she had to the kingdom of God. I was simply overwhelmed by the love, the prayers, and the assistance given to me by the people of Beth Israel. Meanwhile, momentum was building among the Sudanese communities in New Jersey, New York, Ohio, and Washington, D.C.

Soon we found ourselves at the last meeting before the scheduled UN march. The permits were in order, and arrangements were made. But I realized that a spirit of division had crept into our movement, and it had to be addressed.

## Facing the Giants

On the very eve of the historic event of Sudanese exiles gathering together to support the cause of their people, there was a serious lack of solidarity. Many felt that we would get no response from the UN if we called ourselves Christians, especially from the Islamic countries. They felt it would be more expedient to identify ourselves with a political faction. Still others felt that I was simply too young and unable to understand the subtleties of politics.

It was then that Pastor Gary asked to speak to the group. He turned to the Bible and read from 1 Samuel, the story of David's call from the house of Jesse. David was younger and smaller than all of his brothers, but God chose him to do His work. Everyone was surprised that God chose David.

Gary added, "David was young and inexperienced, but he relied completely on God. Everyone was amazed at what God accomplished through him. I think you all will be amazed at what God wants to accomplish here. William is young and he is small of stature. He doesn't have political aspirations, and he isn't involved with any political faction. But the Lord says, it is 'not by might, power, or strength, but by My Spirit.'"

No one spoke, so I stood to offer a final appeal.

"Listen, my fellow Sudanese," I began, "we are

fighting a spiritual battle, and we face a common enemy. We must unite. We all follow a living God and a Savior by whose name we are set free from the bondage of sin and disunity."

I tried to make eye contact with each person in the room, realizing that this would likely be my last chance to keep our movement together.

"I realize there are political and ideological differences within this group, but I ask you to unite under the name of our Lord Jesus," I said. "I will not deny the name of Christ to appease some politicians at the UN. I do not fear men who can kill my body, but I fear God."

Then I laid down the final challenge: If they were with me, I asked them to stand.

For a moment, nobody moved. Then slowly, deliberately, an elderly gentleman rose to his feet. One by one, the men stood as the Spirit convicted them to rise. Before long, the whole group was standing.

"Praise God!" I said loudly, with both joy and relief. I knew that I had just witnessed something miraculous.

Even as tears welled up in my eyes, I knew that the time for tears was past.

After Nehemiah wept, mourned, fasted, and prayed, he knew that God was ready to move. And Nehemiah was there, ready to obey. A sense of calm and resolve spread over the group of men. They were ready to set aside their differences for the greater good. It was time to rebuild the walls.

*Then said I unto them, Ye see the distress that we are in, how Jerusalem lieth waste, and the gates thereof are burned with fire: come, and let us build up the wall of Jerusalem, that we be no more a reproach. Then I told them of the hand of my God which was good upon me; as also the king's words that he had spoken unto me. And they said, Let us rise up and build. So they strengthened their hands for this good work.*

—Nehemiah 2:17–18

# Postscript

ON JULY 31, 1993, over 250 people converged at the United Nations for a peaceful prayer vigil. Several committed Sudanese and American leaders were on hand, including my cousin, Rev. John Moi, former NBA player Manute Bol, Dr. Augustin Ladu, Simon Deng, Gary Selman, Scott Davis, Rev. Glenn Hatfield, and me.

The rally lasted for two hours. It was a breakthrough in that all of the Sudanese participants worked together with all of their hearts. For a little while, at least, we were truly one in the Spirit.

On that same day, a deadly earthquake rocked Khartoum. Was it a sign from God? Only He knows. In the months that followed, however, I worked full time toward transforming the vision that inspired the rally into a full-fledged ministry.

On October 15, 1993, Operation Nehemiah for South Sudan was established as a nonprofit Christian organization. The vision statement was fourfold: spiritual restoration of the church in the Sudan, education of the youth of Sudan, agriculture, and health care development.

Paul Liben, Gary Selman, and I were the first board members. In December of 1993, Beth Israel Messianic Center contributed an office space to house the fledgling ministry.

It was also at this time that my cousin John was due to return to Africa. It was God's plan that he had witnessed the vision for Operation Nehemiah from the very beginning, because he was called to help. He became our first overseas field director with an office in Kampala, Uganda.

In the fall of 1994, the Rev. Michael Longwa, my childhood friend and co-laborer in the Great Commission, became the overseas field director of Operation Nehemiah of Nairobi, Kenya.

Over the next three to four years, Operation Nehemiah was involved in the shipping of over $1 million worth of relief and development supplies to the South Sudan, and that was only the beginning.

For more information about our ministry or to make a tax-exempt gift,* contact us at:

Operation Nehemiah Missions International, Inc.
P.O. Box 2
Cheshire, MA 01225
Website: www.operationsnehemiah.org
Email: levifamily@adelphia.net
Phone: 1-413-354-5128

*We are happy to disclose financial records for your inspection.

# Addendum

## The History of Sudan—Ancient Times to the Present

*THINE EYES have seen my unformed substance;*
*And in Thy book they were all written,*
*The days that were ordained for me,*
*When as yet there was not one of them.*
                                    *—Psalm 139:16 (NASB)*

I don't believe in coincidence. Even in the most tragic moments of human history, God has been at work in the lives of men and nations. In times of war and poverty, as well as peace and prosperity, God always has a plan and a purpose for His children.

There are moments, of course, when that plan doesn't seem to make sense. When the Lord Jesus was mocked, scourged, and crucified, it seemed as though Satan had won. Even Jesus' disciples couldn't understand God's purpose that awful day. But out of the tomb came victory that had been ordained before the foundations of the world. The darkest page in the book of history became the master stroke of God's redemptive plan.

Similarly, recent acts of brutal persecution against Christ's body, the church, have been difficult to understand. Even so, we must not doubt that the battle belongs to the Lord. All of the evil this world can muster is nothing compared to God. He is able to take it, turn it upside down, and use it to further His kingdom. That is the hope that sustains me.

## Africa's Biblical Roots

As both a messianic Hebrew and a native of the war-torn nation of Sudan, I have seen God at work in the histories of both my people and my country. Emerging from the shadow of Egyptian antiquity, the great Nubian kingdoms of Sudan birthed an early Christian dynasty that lasted for nearly ten centuries. Through Roman persecution, Arab conquest, and British rule, Sudan has been "struck down, but not destroyed" (2 Corinthians 4:9 NASB). It is the land of a remnant preserved by God through the millennia.

The recent history of my people in Sudan has been incredibly painful. Intense religious persecution and bitter civil war have ended the lives of millions of people over the past twenty years. Only the Holocaust of World War II has exceeded the scope of the genocide. Political analysts throw up their hands and declare the situation hopeless. In the eyes of the world, Sudan has reason only for despair.

But God has a plan, and He has called me to serve my oppressed Christian brothers and sisters in Sudan and to reach out in love with the message of the gospel to those who persecute them. Even now, God is in control of history, as He has been from the very beginning. And in the very beginning, according to the Bible, God touched the heart of Africa.

Cush, son of Ham, made his home near the joining of the Blue and the White Nile Rivers sometime after the great flood—and long before the written history of man was first set to stone or papyrus. But Cush was not the first to settle there. The second chapter of Genesis indicates that this land inhabited by Noah's grandson originally comprised the western boundaries of Eden. If that is the case, it is possible that Adam and Eve once walked in Africa. Modern archaeologists now have evidence suggesting that the first human beings originated in Africa, lending scientific credence for the first time to her Edenic origins.

Fertile ground and abundant resources in the Nile River valley would have allowed antediluvian society to flourish in prehistoric times, and Cush's progeny filled the region after the flood. The land was, in a very real sense, a cradle of ancient civilization. Great societies of antiquity can trace their roots to the land of Africa. In the days before Nimrod became a mighty hunter, and before the great ziggurat at Babel thrust a defiant stairway to heaven, the land that is now

Sudan was home to established civilizations. As Nimrod's clan migrated north to Assyria, his Cushite forebears remained and prospered in Africa.

The Hamites inhabited the region to the north of Cush known as Egypt. In the days of Egypt's old kingdom, from 2755–2255 B.C., the land of Cush was heavily influenced by her more powerful neighbor to the north. Cush provided Egypt with rich natural resources such as gold, ivory, and human slaves. By 1570 B.C., Cush was largely an Egyptian province.

Although this was a time of great wealth and culture, the Hamites and Cushites had all but forgotten the Creator God of their ancestor Noah. The pharaohs were revered as gods during their lives, and their days were spent preparing for the journey to an afterlife of their own creation. Fabulous tombs and mummified remains of these ancient pharaohs give us a good idea of the religion of that period. Idolatry ruled the lands that once cradled Eden, but God's eternal plan of redemption began to take shape nonetheless.

The *Apiru,* or Hebrew, peoples were Semitic tribes of "foreigners" who settled in northern Africa around 1500 B.C. to escape famine. At first, the Egyptians welcomed these nomadic tribesmen. But as the Hebrews flourished, they became a threat to the rule of the pharaohs. The Egyptian rulers responded to this threat with oppression and slavery. But Yahweh, the powerful God of the monotheistic Hebrews, intended all of this for good.

The Hebrew peoples were eventually delivered from bondage, and the laws and practice of the worship of Yahweh—the one true God—were formally established and recorded by Moses. The stage was being set for the coming of the Hebrew Messiah, who would be for all people. Africa figured prominently in the history of Israel and in the life of Christ.

The Hebrews gained their name in Africa, and they have been a continuous presence on that continent ever since. Waves of new Hebrew immigration occurred after the Assyrian conquest of Israel in the eighth century B.C., and again after the fall of Jerusalem some two hundred years later.

The Bible indicates that Christianity was originally received in the land of Cush in the first century A.D. By this time, the Roman Empire exerted considerable control in the region. The book of Acts describes a meeting between the apostle Philip and a royal eunuch who was returning home to Africa after a pilgrimage to the city of Jerusalem. The eunuch was reading a messianic prophecy from the book of Isaiah when Philip explained to him its meaning— and its fulfillment in the life of Jesus Christ. Immediately, the eunuch stopped his chariot and asked to be baptized in a nearby body of water.

*And when they came up out of the water, the Spirit of the Lord snatched Philip away; and the eunuch saw him no more, but went on his way rejoicing* (Acts 8:39 NASB).

It isn't clear whether the Ethiopian eunuch was a Jew by birth or a proselyte, but the Holy Spirit chose him for a unique encounter with God. He was an important man—in charge of the treasury of

Queen Candace. The title of "Candace" was given to all the queens of Ethiopia in those days. This eunuch would have been headed to the capital city of the kingdom of Meroe, located on the Nile River just north of the confluence of the Blue and the White Niles, in the heart of present-day Sudan. No doubt this influential man brought the good news of the Messiah back to the courts of Queen Candace and to the synagogues of the region. Originally, the message of the Messiah was taken only to Jewish groups, and they became the first Christians.

## From Christ to Islam

The new faith called Christianity spread quickly throughout northern Africa in the first century A.D. The first African church, which is also referred to as the "Old Church" or *"Kanisa Ajuza"* in Arabic, was born in Dunqulah, the capital city of ancient Meroe. Tradition holds that many of these very early believers were converted based on the testimony of the Ethiopian eunuch. It is certain that they helped form the kernel that developed many years later into the Nubian Christian kingdom.

By the end of the second century A.D., the majority of northern Africa was Christian, producing such early church fathers as Origen, Tertullian, and Augustine. It was Tertullian who was credited with the famous quotation: "The blood of the martyrs is the seed of the church." He was well acquainted with martyrdom, because the Romans at the time were killing African Christians at an alarming rate.

But despite persecution, the church grew steadily over the next three hundred years.

Eventually, Nubian royalty declared Christianity the "state" religion. The Nubian-Cushite kingdom was predominantly Christian from A.D. 350 until A.D. 1500, when Muslim conquerors established Islam as the official religion. The Cushite Christians, famous for their skills with the lance, had held off the Islamists since A.D. 649, when the Arabs conquered Egypt. They formed an uneasy truce with the Arabs for several centuries, maintaining the peace with an annual tribute of slaves.

During the twelfth and thirteenth centuries, Arab invasions hammered away at Christian resistance. Great numbers of Nubians were killed or sold into slavery, and the remaining Christians hid in remote areas without any communication with other Christians or the world at large. African Hebrews were also increasingly isolated; some had retreated during Nubian Christian rule, and more sought remote havens as the Muslims advanced. As the Nubians fled, Arab settlers claimed the land and converted church buildings into mosques. The remaining Nubians were absorbed into the new culture through intermarriage and conversion.

In A.D. 1315 a Muslim prince who had Nubian royal blood claimed the throne in Dunqulah. Soon, the Arabs changed the name of the land of Cush to *Sudan,* meaning "the land of the Blacks." Christians and Jews who refused to convert to Islam scattered into the African interior. They ended up in southern Sudan and parts of modern Ethiopia, Libya, and the horn of Africa, where they maintained their faith and their African heritage within tribal groups. Finally, in approximately A.D. 1500, all traces of the Nubian Christian kingdom vanished.

## In and Out of Slavery

After the Muslim conquest of the Christian kingdom of Nubia, several Islamic dynasties arose and fell, and Sudan came under the domination of the Ottoman Turks. By 1820, Turko-Egyptian rule forced churches and synagogues to operate underground due to the strict Islamic orthodoxy that held sway. The *Turkiyah* were greedy and ruthless, exacting exorbitant taxes, ransacking ancient pyramids, and pushing the slave trade into high gear.

Africans who were captured by Arab slave traders were sold to Europeans on the island of Zanzibar, off the coast of modern-day Tanzania. These slaves were exported to Arabia, Europe, and the Americas for forced labor and other abuses.

By this time, slavery had become a destabilizing crisis in Africa. Still, some antislavery voices were emerging in the Western world. William Wilberforce, an influential Brit in the House of Commons, became an important figure in the antislavery movement. A devout Christian, he challenged the logic behind men selling men for profit. He concluded that slavery was an "evil adventure" that must be eliminated at all costs.

Eventually, the abolitionists' ideals prevailed in the courts of law in Great Britain—and through a bloody war in the United States. Slavery was officially abolished in the West, but not in the Islamic world, and not in Sudan.

A coalition of Egyptian and British forces took control of the Sudan in the late nineteenth century. Great Britain was mainly concerned with the preservation of its interest in the Suez Canal, which linked the English to their most valued colony—India. The British immediately saw the problem of religious and ethnic conflict between the North and the South, and they set about to stop it. During colonial rule, the North and South were strictly separated, and Arabs were not allowed into the southern territories. Slave raiding was ended. Soon, missionaries were sent into the South to establish schools, churches, and medical clinics.

When European missionaries finally penetrated what they had in ignorance called "the Dark Continent," they found the fragile remnants of ancient African Christians and tribal Jewry alive and well and living in the Sudan.

As the Europeans worked among previously isolated tribal groups, they found very pious people— even though the influence of orthodoxy had been gone for centuries. Literacy had faded, but oral tradition remained. Many of these people, descended from Christian or Hebrew families, were very receptive to the gospel. After all, Christianity and Judaism had flourished in Africa hundreds of years before they had ever reached the remote and somewhat barbaric peoples of places like Great Britain. So, the "new" message of the missionaries was already understood at some level by many of the Sudanese.

It may be due to the legacy of the slave trade that Westerners today are largely unaware of the spiritual and cultural heritage of the African people. One widely propagated lie during the time of European slave trade was that Cushite blacks were cursed by God and destined for slavery. If anyone at that time had bothered to read his Bible, he would have discovered that it was not Cush who had been cursed but Canaan, his son. No Canaanites remain in modern times; so that curse cannot be applied to any living people group. Even so, the myth of the curse persisted—probably because some people wanted to believe it to justify their immoral actions.

## Preserving the Faith

My family came from an African Hebrew tribal group. We traced our ancestry to the priestly line of Levi, and we had survived for hundreds of years in isolation—with an amazingly well-preserved system of Levitical law and traditions. Circumcision took place on the eighth day, marriage was in the Levitical tradition, and many of our words were Hebrew in origin.

Most of our history had been handed down through the years by oral tradition. From our tribe, and from others like ours, emerged a new and vibrant messianic Jewish population that came to know *Yeshua* (i.e., Jesus) for the first time. But even though a tiny remnant of God's people had been preserved to greet the Western missionaries, all was not well with the spiritual life of Africa. Violent Islamization and tribal witchcraft had taken a toll. A war was being waged in the invisible realm for the souls of the African people.

It was with this great sense of the history of my people—descended from the ancient Hebrews—and the Great Commission of Jesus Christ that I was raised. My land and my people are found in the Genesis account, and both find the beginning of grace in the book of Acts.

Perhaps I shouldn't be surprised that the Enemy is waging one of his most bitter battles in my homeland, among my people. While there is indeed a terrible physical battle going on, the heart of the battle is supernatural. The serpent of old has been at work from Cain's jealous rage to Africa's modern-day massacres, trying to stamp out the people of God's covenants. In doing so, he hopes to defeat the plan of Christ. But the outcome of the conflict has been predetermined, and I am determined to be on the Lord's side.

**Note:** *This chapter only scratches the surface of Sudanese history, which dates from prehistoric times. Scriptural, scholarly, and legendary sources were used. Historical information was taken from the sources below:*

Felder, Cain Hope Ph.D. ed., *The Original African Heritage Study Bible* (KJV), World Bible Publishing, 1993

The Library of Congress Web site, http://lcweb2.loc.gov, keyword Sudan.

ArabNet, http://www.arab.net, keyword Sudan.

*Ancient History Sourcebook:* http://www.fordham.edu, keywords Kush and Meroe.

McEvedy, Colin. *The Penguin Atlas of Ancient History.* New York: Penguin.

Wallis Budge, E. A. trans. *The Kebra Negast,* Cosimo, Inc., 2004.

Malka, Eli S. *Jacob's Children in the Land of the Mahdi: Jews of the Sudan.* Syracuse, N.Y.: Syracuse University Press, 1997.

*The Columbia Encyclopedia,* fifth ed. New York: Columbia University Press, 1994, 1995.

Personal notes of William Levi.

William and Hannah Levi currently reside in rural Massachusetts with their two children, Abijah (2) and Nechemyah (1). They are expecting a third child, Hadassah, in August, 2005. Since 1996, William has been working full-time for Operation Nehemiah Missions as its founder, president and CEO. In collaboration with seven U.S. based directors serving with Operation Nehemiah, he is involved directing development projects in the Sudan from his home office. Hannah is a full-time mother and homemaker setting a godly example for the next generation of young wives and mothers.

Operation Nehemiah is currently focused on rebuilding efforts in the South Sudan, which includes evangelism, construction, food production, health care, and community education.

The Levis are deeply committed to keeping Operation Nehemiah Missions Christ-centered. They are integrating the ministry vision into their family and those who are involved with it to live a life worthy of Christ calling. They endeavor to glorify Christ through raising up another generation of strong, godly children both here in America and in the Sudan.

# The Negro National Anthem

Lift every voice and sing
Till earth and heaven ring,
Ring with the harmonies of Liberty;
Let our rejoicing rise
High as the listening skies,
Let it resound loud as the rolling sea.
Sing a song full of the faith that the dark past has taught us,
Sing a song full of the hope that the present has brought us,
Facing the rising sun of our new day begun
Let us march on till victory is won.

LIFT EVERY VOICE

So begins the Black National Anthem, written by James Weldon Johnson in 1900. Lift Every Voice is the name of the joint imprint of The Institute for Black Family Development and Moody Publishers.

Our vision is to advance the cause of Christ through publishing African-American Christians who educate, edify, and disciple Christians in the church community through quality books written for African Americans.

Since 1988, the Institute for Black Family Development, a 501(c)(3) nonprofit Christian organization, has been providing training and technical assistance for churches and Christian organizations. The Institute for Black Family Development's goal is to become a premier trainer in leadership development, management, and strategic planning for pastors, ministers, volunteers, executives, and key staff members of churches and Christian organizations. To learn more about The Institute for Black Family Development, write us at:

15151 Faust
Detroit, Michigan 48223

Since 1894, *Moody Publishers* has been dedicated to equip and motivate people to advance the cause of Christ by publishing evangelical Christian literature and other media for all ages, around the world. Because we are a ministry of the Moody Bible Institute of Chicago, a portion of the proceeds from the sale of this book go to train the next generation of Christian leaders. If we may serve you in any way in your spiritual journey toward understanding Christ and the Christian life, please contact us at:

820 N. LaSalle Blvd.
Chicago, Illinois 60610
www.moodypublishers.com

## THE BIBLE OR THE AXE TEAM

**ACQUIRING EDITOR**
Cynthia Ballenger

**COPY EDITOR**
Ed Gilbreath

**COVER DESIGN**
WinePress & Jaxon Communications

**INTERIOR DESIGN**
BlueFrog Design

**PRINTING AND BINDING**
Bethany Press International

*The typeface for the text of this book is*
***Sabon***